# Larkin's Dulcimer Book

*By* Larkin Bryant

*For Beginning and Intermediate*
*Dulcimer Players*

*With Illustrations By*

Peg Nichols
*and*
Larkin Bryant

**IVORY PALACES** Music Publishing Company, Inc.   3141 Spottswood Avenue • Memphis, Tennessee • 38111

# Credits

I want to thank the many friends who helped and supported me throughout the writing of this book.  Thanks, most of all to my patient and loving husband, David; to Jack, my publisher, who's responsible for the book happening; to Lydia and Phyllis, who laboriously typed and retyped the tabs and text; to Peggy Nichols Root, a very talented artist who spent many hours drawing hands and the musicians from photographs; to Gladys Kozik for doing the cover design and layout; to Julia Wallis for the title design; to Ray Allen, folklorist at the Center For Southern Folklore, Memphis, TN, and Dr. Maurice Crouse, picker extraordinaire and Professor of American History at Memphis State University, who helped me with the historical notes; to my proofreaders, Frankie Adkins, Betty Bridges, Rosamond Campbell, Carol Lévy, Maurice Crouse and Shirley McRae; to Elliott Hancock of the Ozark Folk Center for writing the Foreword; and to all my students for their invaluable suggestions and support.

Book layout and design: Larkin Bryant
Front cover photo: Bonnie Carol
Back cover photo: David Bryant
Music typography: Ivory Palaces
Printing: Diamond Printing Co., Memphis


First printing July, 1982; second printing March, 1983; third printing October, 1983; fourth printing October, 1984; fifth printing October, 1985; sixth printing October, 1986

Copyright © 1982 by Ivory Palaces Music Publishing Co.,Inc., 3141 Spottswood Ave., Memphis, TN 38111.  All rights reserved.  International copyright secured No part of this publication, including illustrations, may be reproduced or transmitted in any form or by any means, electronic or mechanical, including photocopy, recording, or any information storage and retrieval system, without permission in writing from the publisher.

ISBN  0-943644-00-3

Library of Congress Card Catalog Number: 82-84550

**IVORY PALACES**
TM
**Music Publishing Company, Inc.**
3141 Spottswood Avenue • Memphis, Tennessee • 38111

This book is lovingly dedicated to the memory of
Robert L. Dickey
an old-time dulcimer player and builder,
fiddler, guitar picker and singer
who, along with his wife, Myra,
inspired many young pickers
to preserve and carry on
the heritage of our traditional
old-time music.

"People have often remarked that while the dulcimer is playing it seems as if someone were singing in the background.  To me it is my grandfather singing *The Unclouded Day* or *Amazing Grace*. To others, something else perhaps, but certainly to all who listen seriously it is the song of The Everlasting Hills."

-Robert L. Dickey

# Contents

APPENDIX 91-103

About musical time, note values, measures and time signatures 91,92 · How to read the dulcimer tablature 93 · Playing back-up chords to accompany other instruments 94 · Tuning dulcimer to play in other keys, especially C, E and F 95 · D/A/D' Chord chart 96 · D/A/C Chord chart 97 · D/A/G Chord chart 98 · D/A/A Chord chart 99,100 · Fret chart for making your own chords 100 · Quick reference chart for modes and tunings in the book 101,102 · How to tune to C, E and F with the guitar 101 · Possible modes and keys in D/A/A  D/A/G  D/A/C  D/A/D' 102 · Bibliography 103 ·

SONGS

# Foreword

Larkin Bryant has a large and enthusiastic following in the Memphis, Tennessee area where she conducts dulcimer classes through the Continuing Education Department of Memphis State University. Although the reputation of Memphis' First Lady of the Dulcimer is well established in her hometown, Larkin has only recently been getting recognition on the national level. Therefore, I consider this a privilege to be given the opportunity to assist in introducing Larkin Bryant to a wider and what I know will be a very receptive audience.

Those of us in the dulcimer community in Mountain View, Arkansas, have watched and delighted in Larkin's musical development. It was here, in 1973, with the purchase of a McSpadden dulcimer from the Dulcimer Shoppe that Larkin began a relationship with the instrument that has now become a career. At the Ozark Folk Center in Mountain View, Larkin won her first dulcimer contest in 1979. She went on to place second in the National Championships in Winfield, Kansas, that same year. In concert, Larkin draws primarily on music from American and British tradition, but her repertoire includes contemporary selections as well.

Larkin is an accomplished musician who can also relate to the experiences of a rank beginner or a struggling intermediate. This rare blend has made her an exceptional teacher. The materials used in *Larkin's Dulcimer Book* were developed for use with her students in the Memphis State program and arranged into a format which can be followed without a personal instructor, even by persons without previous musical training. Beginners and intermediates alike will benefit from this step-by-step manual and the tape supplement. In short, the materials presented here have been tested and proven in the classroom.

I predict that *Larkin's Dulcimer Book* will become accepted as the basic instruction manual for the Mountain Dulcimer. Both in matters of content and style, this book is the next best thing to having an instructor present, whether you are a pure novice or looking for help in more advanced techniques. I can even envision *Larkin's Dulcimer Book* being used by teachers as a text for their beginning and intermediate students.


ELLIOTT HANCOCK
Ozark Folk Center
Mountain View, Arkansas

Dear Dulcimer Friend,

It is my hope that this book will nurture you in the style of my friend,
the late Robert Dickey, to whom this book is dedicated.  Mr. Dickey always used
to "shove" them out on stage...the new pickers, young and old.  If they were
pretty good, he'd ask them to join the Wildwood Rhythms, his bluegrass band.
From then on, he'd nurture them and guide them and teach them to love and
respect the old-time music.  Likewise, I hope this book will guide you in
learning to play the dulcimer, and teach you something about traditional music
along the way.

*Larkin's Dulcimer Book* will give you the tools you need to make music:
basic and intermediate techniques, plus songs that use those techniques.  As
you work through the book, your playing skills will gradually develop.  The
companion tape is co-ordinated with the text so that all techniques, tunings and
songs are clearly demonstrated.  Whenever you see this symbol ⬚⬚ , refer to
the tape for an example.

Take your time and learn each skill before you continue on to the next one.
I hope you have fun learning to play the dulcimer.  It's truly a wonderful
companion whether you play simple tunes or more difficult pieces.

*Larkin*

# Introduction

WHERE DOES THE DULCIMER COME FROM?

The fretted Appalachian dulcimer, or mountain dulcimer, is an American folk instrument that came out of the Southern Appalachian Mountains.  The delicate strains of this handcrafted instrument have been heard in those hills for about one hundred and fifty years, though their origin remains a mystery.  Were they fashioned after Old World instruments faintly remembered, or were they influenced by instruments then in existence?  We do know that the Pennsylvania Germans migrated into West Virginia and Virginia in the early 1700's bringing with them their knowledge of the German fretted zither, which greatly resembles the dulcimer.  Whatever its origin, as Robert Dickey once said, the dulcimer is certainly the *"song of the Everlasting Hills."*

The word dulcimer comes from the Latin word "dulcis" (sweet) and the Greek word "melos" (sound), and is mentioned in the King James Version of the Bible.  Various unrelated instruments down through the ages have been called by this name.

MODES AND THE DULCIMER

Look at the arrangement of the frets on the dulcimer.  Notice the spaces between the frets.  Some of the spaces are wide while others are narrow.  This is one of the reasons that the dulcimer is different from other fretted instruments.  If the dulcimer were fretted like a guitar, for example, there would be a fret placed in the middle of each wide space on the fretboard.

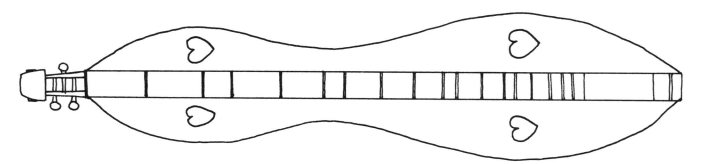

The dulcimer has this odd fret scale because fretted zithers are believed to go back to medieval times when modal scales were in common use.

## WHAT IS A MODE?

A mode is, very simply, a type of scale. Do you remember singing, *do, re mi, fa, sol, la, ti, do* in school? Well, you were singing a scale or mode. It is possible to play seven different modal scales on the dulcimer. Each mode has its own mood or feeling. Some modes are happy and full of frolic; some modes are haunting, while others are full of sadness. You can find the different modes by starting at different places in the *do, re, mi* scale. The major scale beginning on *do* is called the Ionian mode (all modes have Greek names). If you begin the scale with the second note, *re*, and sing until you come to *re* again, you will have the Dorian mode. If you sing from *sol* to *sol*, you'll have the Mixolydian mode and from *la* to *la*, the Aeolian mode. These are the four commonly played modes and the ones that are stressed in this book. The three less common modes are the Lydian, *fa* to *fa*, the Phrygian, *mi* to *mi*, and the Locrian, *ti* to *ti*.

## WHERE DO THE MODES START ON THE DULCIMER?

Look at the illustration to see where each mode begins. Find the beginning fret number for the Ionian, Dorian, Mixolydian and Aeolian modes. Memorize where each mode begins.

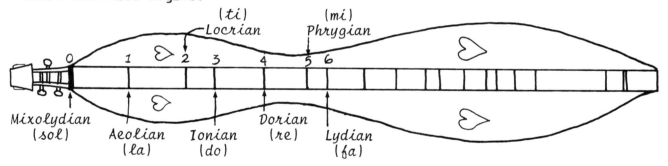

## A BIT ABOUT MODAL MUSIC

An unaccompanied melody is the oldest form of modal music. Later, a drone was added, consisting of one or two harmonizing notes that were played to accompany the melody. Instruments of the fretted zither family were designed to play this type of modal music. Centuries later, mountain style dulcimers would be played in much the same way with the melody noted on the treble string (or unison strings on a four string dulcimer) and bass and middle strings played as drones.

# Part I: Getting Started

## THE ANATOMY OF THE DULCIMER

There are certain parts of the dulcimer you need to know about before starting to play.  Since you'll be learning songs by fret numbers, be sure to check on the following optional frets to keep you from playing the tablature incorrectly.

ZERO FRET  Not all dulcimers have this fret and it is not used in playing.
   It functions as a nut.  The "0" found in the tablature stands for "open",
   which means that the string is not held down.

THE 6½ AND 13½ FRETS  These are new additions to the fret scale, added in the
   Fifties to give extra notes not possible in the original fret scale.  The
   6½ is more common than the 13½.  Be sure to count these frets by their
   proper names, if you have them, so your numbering won't be off.

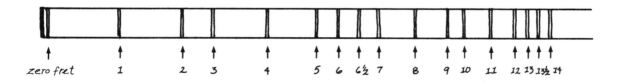

zero fret      1      2   3      4      5  6  6½ 7      8    9  10  11   12 13 13½ 14

BASS STRING  The lowest pitched string.

MIDDLE STRING  Placed between the bass and the treble string(s).

SINGLE TREBLE STRING  Three string dulcimers have a single treble string.

UNISON TREBLE STRINGS  Most four string dulcimers have two treble strings
   strung closely enough together so that they can be fretted as one string.

   (This book assumes that you have a three string dulcimer or a four string
   dulcimer tuned with unison treble strings.  Some four string dulcimers
   have a convertible nut and bridge so that they can be played two ways,
   with unison treble strings or with four equally spaced strings.)

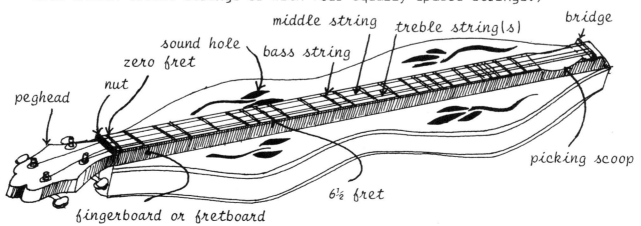

## HOW TO HOLD THE DULCIMER IN YOUR LAP

Sit down, as
illustrated.
Make sure the dulcimer
is level in your lap
so that it won't tip
forward.
Position the 1st fret
over your left knee
and the strumming end
next to your hip.
Place your left foot slightly
ahead of your right foot.
Be sure your arms have
freedom to move.

Since both dulcimers and people come in many sizes, you may have to make some slight adjustments.  The main object is to have the dulcimer balanced so that it won't wobble or tip while you play.  A chamois works wonderfully to keep the dulcimer from sliding across your lap.

## PLAYING WITH A NOTER

The easiest way to play the dulcimer is with a noter and this is the old-time mountain way. OO  Ex.1  Tunes are played on the treble string(s) by sliding the noter up and down the fretboard while the strumming hand strums across all the strings.  You can make a noter from a 4" length of 3/8" dowel or use a popsickle stick.

Hold the noter between your thumb and index finger, as shown. Press the noter down on the treble string(s). If you have unison treble strings, place the noter on both of them. Do not touch the middle string with the noter. The side of your index finger slides up and down the edge of the fingerboard keeping the noter in place.

To play notes, press the noter down just to the <u>left</u> of the frets you want to play (about 1/8"-1/4" to the left).  The 3rd fret is shown being noted. The "whiney" sound of noter style playing is produced by keeping the noter on the treble strings as you move up and down the fingerboard.

## FRETTING WITH YOUR FINGERS

More and more people are playing the dulcimer with their fingers since this style allows you to use fancy finger techniques and chording. In the beginning, it's easiest to play with one finger or thumb so that you can concentrate on finding the right frets. Once you've learned how to play you can use as many fingers as you like. I began to fret notes with my thumb as shown below. 🔲 Ex.2

Use the SIDE of the thumb to press down on the treble string(s). Be sure to fret unison treble strings as if they were one string. To fret a note, press the thumb just to the left (about 1/8"-1/4") of the desired fret (3rd fret shown). Slide the thumb up and down the fretboard from fret to fret to play tunes. You can also fret with your index finger, using the end for fretting. You may have to cut your nails to play this way.

Your fingers will be tender from fretting the strings the first few weeks. Practice a little bit every day and your fingers will gradually toughen up.

### TIPS ON TUNING

If you have never played a stringed instrument, then tuning will be your first goal. Although tuning may not come overnight, if you've done some singing or have played any kind of musical instrument, you're already on first base. If not, be willing to spend some time training your ears to hear musical tones. I have read that there is no such thing as being tone deaf, but there are definitely people with untrained ears.

Try to tune when it's quiet as any kind of noise will greatly hinder your ability to hear the tones. If you can't find a quiet place, hold the dulcimer next to your ear as you pluck the strings. It's like hearing the tones through a sound system!

Here are the steps to follow when tuning a dulcimer string:

1. Hear the pitch you want to arrive at, either by plucking that note on another string of the dulcimer, or by sounding a tuning device or another musical instrument.

2. Pluck the string you are tuning to see if by chance it is the same as the pitch you want to arrive at. If so, you need go no further (lucky you!) If not, however, you must now decide whether your string is too high or too low.*

3. If the string is too high, lower it until it exactly matches the pitch you want to arrive at. If it's too low, raise it until you arrive at the desired pitch. A good way to do this is to repeatedly pluck the string you are tuning and alternate it with the pitch you want to arrive at until they are the same.

*If you can't tell whether the string is too high or too low, use the old trial and error method: if the pitches get closer together, you guessed right; if they get further apart, try going the other direction.

## HOW DO YOU TUNE A DULCIMER?

Since the dulcimer is a modal instrument and has *no standard tuning,* there are a lot of different ways to tune the strings. This book teaches four tunings that put you in four different modes. These four tunings are good for playing a wealth of songs.

## TUNING THE DULCIMER TO A CERTAIN PITCH

The tunings in this book are given so that each of the four modes will be pitched in a D scale; that is, each mode will begin and end with the note D. This simplifies tuning quite a bit. *By keeping each mode in D, only the treble string(s) need to be re-tuned when going from one tuning to another.* Page 101 in this book has instructions for tuning to C, E, and F.

## TUNING THE DULCIMER TO ITSELF

Although the dulcimer may be tuned to pitches other than D, if tuned too high, the strings may break, and if tuned too low, they may sound like rubber bands. To tune the dulcimer to itself, just pick a random note for the bass string and tune the other strings from the bass note, following the instructions for each dulcimer tuning.

## WHAT'S THE DIFFERENCE BETWEEN A MODE AND A TUNING?

A *mode* is a kind of scale, remember? When the dulcimer strings are tuned to certain related pitches, it's said to be in a *tuning.* Once the strings are tuned, certain modes can be played. A tuning is not a mode and a mode is not a tuning!

### THE IONIAN MODE

The Ionian mode is an excellent mode to begin with because so many familiar songs can be played in it. It's the most joyful sounding of all the modes and is the equivalent of our modern major scale. The Ionian mode begins at the 3rd fret on the treble string(s) and continues up to the 10th fret (be sure to leave out the 6½ fret if you have it, since it's not part of the scale).

### IONIAN MODE

| | | | | | | | | |
|---|---|---|---|---|---|---|---|---|
| The DO scale | do | re | mi | fa | sol | la | ti | do |
| Frets | 3 | 4 | 5 | 6 | 7 | 8 | 9 | 10 |
| Note names in D Ionian scale | D | E | F♯ | G | A | B | C♯ | D |

Here's the traditional way to tune the dulcimer so that you can play tunes in the Ionian mode:

TUNING TO 
**D** *bass string*
**A** *middle string*
**A** *treble string(s)*

⬚⬚ Ex.3: $\begin{smallmatrix}D\\A\\A\end{smallmatrix}$ Tuning

1. Tune the bass string to low D, getting the note from the tape or by tuning to low D on the piano or guitar as shown below, or from a guitar pitch pipe. If you want to tune the dulcimer to itself, pick a note at random, making sure it's a low sounding note with good tone, and follow the next steps.

2. Fret the bass string at the 4th fret and tune the OPEN (unfretted) middle string to sound the same as the FRETTED bass string.

3. Tune the OPEN treble string(s) to sound the same as the OPEN middle string. If you have two treble strings, begin by tuning the inside treble, then the outside treble. When these two strings are perfectly tuned, they will sound like one string when strummed.

When you're through tuning all the strings, strum across them to hear if you have a harmonious sound. If not, go through each step again, listening carefully and taking lots of time.

Here are the notes:

On the piano:

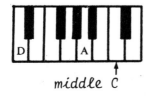

*middle C*

On the guitar:

D　　　　　A　　　　　A

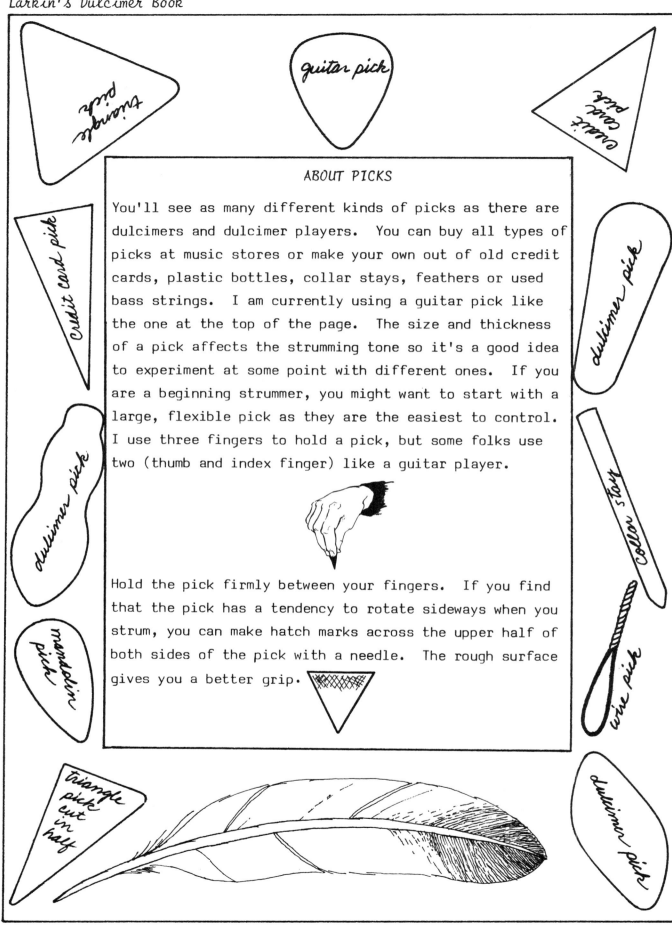

## ABOUT PICKS

You'll see as many different kinds of picks as there are dulcimers and dulcimer players. You can buy all types of picks at music stores or make your own out of old credit cards, plastic bottles, collar stays, feathers or used bass strings. I am currently using a guitar pick like the one at the top of the page. The size and thickness of a pick affects the strumming tone so it's a good idea to experiment at some point with different ones. If you are a beginning strummer, you might want to start with a large, flexible pick as they are the easiest to control. I use three fingers to hold a pick, but some folks use two (thumb and index finger) like a guitar player.

Hold the pick firmly between your fingers. If you find that the pick has a tendency to rotate sideways when you strum, you can make hatch marks across the upper half of both sides of the pick with a needle. The rough surface gives you a better grip.

triangle pick

guitar pick

credit card pick

credit card pick

dulcimer pick

dulcimer pick

collar stay

mandolin pick

wire pick

triangle pick cut in half

dulcimer pick

## WHERE TO STRUM

Most dulcimers have a picking scoop which keeps the pick from wearing out the fingerboard underneath it. Some dulcimer players strum a little to the left of the picking scoop because of the tone and comfortable arm position, but it's easy to scar your fingerboard this way.

Notice how the sound quality changes depending on where you strum. I recommend the position illustrated below for general strumming.

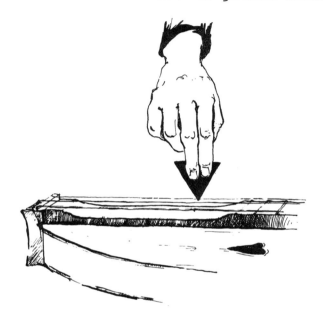

It's nice to practice strumming back and forth across the open strings until your strumming action becomes natural. Be sure to strum lightly across the strings to get the delicate sound that's characteristic of dulcimer music. If you use too much force, you'll get too much pick noise. To get a better tone, allow only the tip end of the pick to strike the strings.

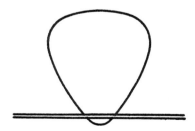

If you want more volume, use a smaller, thicker pick.

## WHICH DIRECTION TO STRUM FIRST

I start my strumming action with an IN strum, toward the body. Traditionally, dulcimer players start their strumming this way. However, lots of dulcimer players today start by strumming OUT, away from the body, which may seem more natural because of its similarity to guitar strumming. You should strum whichever way sounds the best to you.

The beginning strum direction is important because it's your dominant strum. It's like being right or left-handed. I call this dominant strum the *LEAD* strum which is symbolized by a dash(-) in the exercises and the tablature. If you start by strumming IN, always read the dash(-) as an IN strum. If you start by strumming OUT, read the dash(-) as an OUT strum. Do a series of *LEAD* strums. Watch the movement of your hand as it strums the *LEAD* strum, then returns *silently* back across the strings before playing the next *LEAD* strum.

The *LEAD* strum:  - - - - - - - - - - - - - - - - - - - - - - -

## PLAYING A SIMPLE SONG WITH THE LEAD STRUM

The very easiest way to strum a simple song is with the *LEAD* strum, strumming once for each note. Listen to the tape to hear how the song goes. Before you play the song, be sure you've checked to see if you have the 6½ fret (see p. 5) to avoid playing some fret numbers incorrectly. To read the tablature, follow the fret numbers above the words. Be sure to strum across all the strings as you play the melody on the treble string(s). The asterisk(*) shows you where the beat falls. See the notes on musical time in the back of the book.

Copyright © 1982 **IVORY PALACES** Music Publishing Company, Inc. 3141 Spottswood Avenue • Memphis, Tennessee • 38111
All rights reserved, including the right to photocopy.

## STRUMMING BACK AND FORTH: THE LEAD/RETURN STRUM

When you strum back and forth, you should start with the *LEAD* strum, followed by a strum in the opposite direction, which I'll call the *RETURN* strum. Think of one *LEAD* strum and one *RETURN* strum as a unit symbolized in the exercises and tablature by two dots ( . . ). If you start by strumming IN, then always read the first dot as an IN strum and the next dot as an OUT strum. If you start with an OUT strum, always read the first dot as an OUT strum and the next dot as an IN strum. For example:

```
                   IN OUT IN OUT                      OUT IN OUT IN
IN strummers:       ·   ·   ·   ·     OUT strummers:   ·   ·   ·   ·
```

### SOME STRUMMING AND FRETTING EXERCISES USING THE L/R STRUM

1. Try doing a series of *LEAD/RETURN* (L/R) strums, tapping your foot on the beat marks(*). Accent the *LEAD* strum that's over the beat mark by strumming a little harder. 🔲 Ex.4

```
accent       >         >         >         >
L/R strum    . . . . . . . . . . . . . . . .
beat         *         *         *         *
```

2. Play the Ionian scale, changing fret numbers on every beat(*). Don't forget to tap your foot. Notice that the fret numbers change on a *LEAD* strum. 🔲 Ex.5

```
accent         >       >       >       >       >       >       >       >
fret numbers   3       4       5       6       7       8       9       10
L/R strum      . . . . . . . . . . . . . . . . . . . . . . . . . . . . . .
beat           *       *       *       *       *       *       *       *
```

3. Play the Ionian scale, changing fret numbers every time you do a *LEAD* strum. Accent every fret change. 🔲 Ex.6

```
accent         >   >   >   >   >   >   >   >   >   >   >   >   >   >   >   >
fret numbers   3   4   5   6   7   8   9   10  10  9   8   7   6   5   4   3
L/R strum      . . . . . . . . . . . . . . . . . . . . . . . . . . . . . . . .
beat           *       *       *       *       *       *       *       *
```

Usually, the melody is played with *LEAD* strums.  If the melody contains some very fast notes, however, it's easier to use the *LEAD* strum as well as the *RETURN* strum to play them.  Play the Ionian scale quickly, alternating *LEAD* and *RETURN* strums for each melody note.  Ex.7

| accent | | > | > | > | > | | > | > | > | > | | | | | |
|---|---|---|---|---|---|---|---|---|---|---|---|---|---|---|---|
| fret numbers | 3 | 4 | 5 | 6 | 7 | 8 | 9 | 10 | 10 | 9 | 8 | 7 | 6 | 5 | 4 | 3 |
| L/R strum | . | . | . | . | . | . | . | . | . | . | . | . | . | . | . | . |
| beat | * | | | * | | | * | | | * | | | | | |

## PLAYING AUNT RHODIE WITH THE L/R STRUM

Listen to the tape of *Aunt Rhodie* played with the *L/R* strum, tapping your foot as you listen and following along with the tablature.  Play *Aunt Rhodie* with the *L/R* strum until you can do it without looking at the book.  Try to learn all the songs "by heart" this way.

# Go Tell Aunt Rhodie
### Ionian Mode

D
A  tuning
A

arr. Larkin Bryant

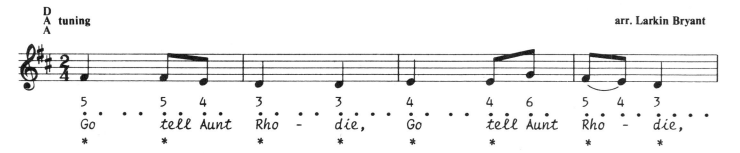

5 · · · 5 4 3 · · 3 · · 4 4 6 5 4 3 · · ·
Go    tell Aunt Rho - die,  Go    tell Aunt Rho - die,
*       *      *        *       *       *          *         *

7 · · · 7 6 5 · 3 3 4 6 5 4 3 · · ·
Go    tell Aunt Rho -- die the old grey goose is dead. · ·
*       *      *        *       *       *          *         *

Copyright © 1982 **IVORY PALACES** Music Publishing Company, Inc.  3141 Spottswood Avenue • Memphis, Tennessee • 38111
All rights reserved, including the right to photocopy.

## THE BASIC ALL PURPOSE DULCIMER STRUM

The *BASIC* dulcimer strum has been handed down to us from the old-time mountain players and it's good for any tune that has a "walking" type beat ($\frac{2}{4}$ or $\frac{4}{4}$). This strum has lots of variations, but we'll begin with the basic one, which is made by combining the *LEAD* strum with the *L/R* strum. The symbol for the *BASIC* strum used in the exercises and tablature is a dash and two dots (- . . ). Listen to this strum on the tape before you try it.

The *BASIC* dulcimer strum sounds like you're saying: "Sing Sis-ter, Sing Sis-ter"
                                                      - . . - . .

Remember that the dash *and* the first dot are always done in the *LEAD* strumming direction. For example:

```
                    IN IN OUT    IN IN OUT                       OUT OUT IN   OUT OUT IN
     IN strummers:   -  . .       -  . .      OUT strummers:      -   . .      -   . .
```

Try a series of *BASIC* dulcimer strums. Play slowly and evenly until you get the hang of it. Place the accent on the first *LEAD* strum. [OO] Ex.8

```
accent         >     >     >     >     >     >     >     >     >     >     >
basic strum    - . - . - . - . - . - . - . - . - . - . - .
beat           *     *     *     *     *     *     *     *     *     *     *
```

You have just done the basic dulcimer strum! Does it feel like patting your head and rubbing your tummy? Don't worry if it does because lots of beginners feel just like you do. You must PRACTICE THIS BASIC STRUM OVER AND OVER UNTIL YOU CAN PLAY IT EASILY, WITHOUT THINKING ABOUT IT! Know it so well that you can have a conversation while strumming.

## BASIC STRUM EXERCISES

The following exercises should help you play *Bile Them Cabbage* with the BASIC strum.

1. Play the Ionian scale, changing fret numbers each time you repeat the BASIC strum pattern. ▣ Ex.9

```
fret numbers   3     4     5     6     7     8     9    10
basic strum   - . . - . . - . . - . . - . . - . . - . . - . .
beat          *     *     *     *     *     *     *     *
```

2. Play the Ionian scale, changing fret numbers for every LEAD strum direction. ▣ Ex.10

```
fret numbers   3 4   5 6   7 8   9 10  10 9  8 7   6 5   4 3
basic strum   - . . - . . - . . - . . - . . - . . - . . - . .
beat          *     *     *     *     *     *     *     *
```

### "BILE THEM CABBAGE": A FAST TUNE PLAYED WITH THE BASIC STRUM

Listen to the tape until you are familiar with the tune. Notice how the strumming fits in. As you listen to the tape, follow along with the written tablature and tap your foot with the beat. Play the song slowly and evenly until it's easy to play it fast. *Never force your speed.*

The capital letters above the music notation are chord names so that another instrument such as a guitar can play with you. To tune the dulcimer and guitar together, see *Tuning to* D A A p. 12. ▣

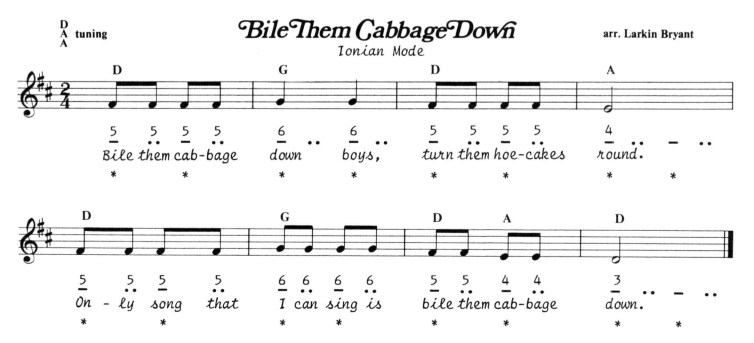

Copyright © 1982 IVORY PALACES Music Publishing Company, Inc. 3141 Spottswood Avenue • Memphis, Tennessee • 38111
All rights reserved, including the right to photocopy.

19

Some of the songs in this book have harmony parts written out. The harmony part can be played by another dulcimer player while you play the melody, or it can be used as a dulcimer accompaniment to your singing.

# Bile Them Cabbage Down

*Harmony Part for Second Dulcimer*

arr. Larkin Bryant

D A A tuning

Bile them cab-bage down boys, turn them hoe-cakes round.

On - ly song that I can sing is bile them cab-bage down.

1. Bile them cabbage down boys,
   Turn them hoecakes round.
   Only song that I can sing is
   Bile them cabbage down.

2. Raccoon has a bushy tail,
   Possum's tail is bare.
   Rabbit's got no tail at all
   But a little bitty bunch of hair.

3. Possum up a 'simmon tree,
   Raccoon on the ground.
   Raccoon says to the possum,
   "Won't you shake them 'simmons down?"

4. Jaybird died with the whoopin' cough,
   Sparrow died with the colic.
   Along come the frog with a fiddle on his back,
   Inquirin' his way to the frolic.

Copyright © 1982 **IVORY PALACES** Music Publishing Company, Inc. 3141 Spottswood Avenue • Memphis, Tennessee • 38111
All rights reserved, including the right to photocopy.

## VARIATIONS TO THE BASIC STRUM

In order to make tunes more interesting, the BASIC strum can be given lots of variations and accents. These variations come naturally after you've been playing awhile. The tunes in *Larkin's Dulcimer Book* have strum guides to help you if you're having trouble with strumming or with the rhythm of the tunes. These strum guides are only suggestions. (Remember that tunes can be strummed many different ways: there's no one correct way as long as you have good rhythm.)

Practice the following variations by playing them over and over.

Variation 1  [OO] Ex.11  strum - . . - -  Sounds like you're saying:
                        beat * * "Red Fid-dle Sing Sing"

Variation 2  [OO] Ex.12  strum . . - . -  Sounds like you're saying:
                        beat * * "Pep-per-mint Pep-per-mint"

Variation 3  [OO] Ex.13  strum - . . . . . . Sounds like you're saying:
                        beat * * "Sing Mis-ter Mis-sis-sip-pi"

The next two variations are the BASIC strum and the L/R strum with different accents.

[OO] Ex.14 accent > >       [OO] Ex.15 accent > >
     strum - . . - . .           strum . . . . . . . .
     beat * *                    beat * *

There are many more possibilities for strum variations in 2/4 and 4/4 time not listed here. Try each strum variation on an easy tune like *Bile Them Cabbage*. Notice how different strums can change the sound of a tune.

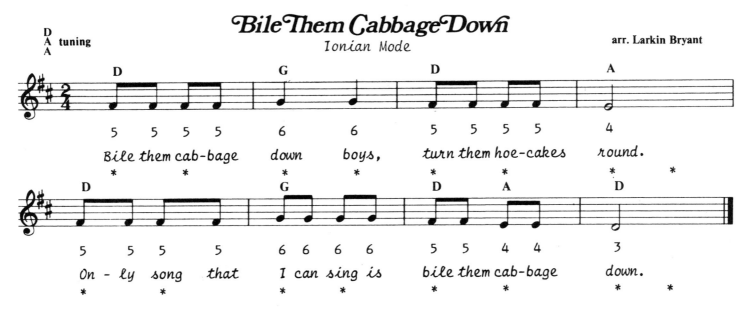

**Bile Them Cabbage Down**
*Ionian Mode*
arr. Larkin Bryant

Copyright © 1982 **IVORY PALACES** Music Publishing Company, Inc. 3141 Spottswood Avenue • Memphis, Tennessee • 38111
All rights reserved, including the right to photocopy.

## PLAYING AUNT RHODIE WITH A COMBINATION OF STRUMS

As your strumming becomes an unconscious motion, you'll begin to combine the strum variations like this arrangement of *Aunt Rhodie*. Remember that these strum guides are only one way to do the song. Notice the long dash(————) at the end of the song. It means that you let the last *LEAD* strum ring until the sound "dies" naturally. This type of strum makes a good ending. 

# Go Tell Aunt Rhodie
### Ionian Mode

DAA tuning

arr. Larkin Bryant

# Go Tell Aunt Rhodie
### Harmony Part for Second Dulcimer

2. The one she's been saving,
The one she's been saving,
The one she's been saving,
To make a feather bed.

3. She died in the millpond,
She died in the millpond,
She died in the millpond,
A-standing on her head.

4. She left nine little goslins,
She left nine little goslins,
She left nine little goslins,
To scratch for their own bread.

Copyright © 1982 **IVORY PALACES** Music Publishing Company, Inc. 3141 Spottswood Avenue • Memphis, Tennessee • 38111
All rights reserved, including the right to photocopy.

Skip To My Lou uses a variety of strum patterns. Notice how the strums fit the rhythm of the words and how strum variation 2 is used to play the fast melody notes in measures 2, 4 and 6.

2. Pretty as a redbird, prettier too,
Pretty as a redbird, prettier too,
Pretty as a redbird, prettier too,
Skip to my Lou my darlin'.

3. Can't get a redbird, bluebird'll do,
Can't get a redbird, bluebird'll do,
Can't get a redbird, bluebird'll do,
Skip to my Lou my darlin'.

Copyright © 1982 IVORY PALACES Music Publishing Company, Inc. 3141 Spottswood Avenue • Memphis, Tennessee • 38111
All rights reserved, including the right to photocopy.

## GETTING AWAY FROM ONE-FINGER PLAYING

If you've gotten to the point where you are comfortable strumming and fretting, you're probably ready to use more than one finger to play the melody. As in strumming, there's no one way to do fingering. You'll find that dulcimer players have their own systems for fingering which fit the tunings and chords they use. As long as you're not playing chords, fingering usually isn't a problem unless the tune goes very quickly and hops all up and down the fingerboard.

Most tunes can be played easily by using the ring finger (R) and thumb (T), or ring finger and index finger (I). Here is how it works: if a tune has jumps of three frets, such as 5th fret to the 3rd fret, put your thumb or index finger on 5 and your ring finger on 3. See how your hand and fingers naturally reach this distance? Now, move that same hand position UP the fretboard to the 5th and 7th frets. Now, move DOWN to the 4th and 2nd frets. When you see a jump of several frets, move your hand so it's positioned above those frets and use those two fingers. When the frets are right next to one another, you can slide which-ever finger happens to be there just like you've been doing. Each song has a different fret arrangement and fingering must be tailored to it. As you learn chords, you will begin using the other fingers, but concentrate on playing smooth-ly with two fingers for now.

*Skip To My Lou* is an excellent example of the fingering just suggested. It has the fingering written out for ring finger (R) and thumb (T). You can substi-tute the index finger for the thumb, if you prefer. Remember to place your hand above the frets.

Copyright © 1982 **IVORY PALACES** Music Publishing Company, Inc. 3141 Spottswood Avenue • Memphis, Tennessee • 38111
All rights reserved, including the right to photocopy.

In *Holy Manna* some notes go below the first note of the Ionian scale (3rd fret). "O" means that you strum or pluck the open or unfretted string. Listen to the tape of *Holy Manna* even if you know the hymn so that you can get the feel for this lively arrangement, inspired by Robert L. Dickey. D.C. means to go back to the beginning. The :|| sign means repeat the preceding section of music. 👓

# Holy Manna
### Ionian Mode

arr. Larkin Bryant

Copyright © 1982 **IVORY PALACES** Music Publishing Company, Inc.   3141 Spottswood Avenue • Memphis, Tennessee • 38111
All rights reserved, including the right to photocopy.

## HISTORICAL NOTES

### GO TELL AUNT RHODIE

The dear old aunt in this nursery jingle has gone by many names such as *Patsy*, *Tabby*, *Abby* and *Nancy*, but the story of the old grey goose remains the same. The song is widespread all over America in towns as well as in the countryside. The tune is known as *Greenville* or *Rousseau's Dream* and was published as a piano solo about 1818, according to George Jackson.*

### BILE THEM CABBAGE DOWN

*Bile Them Cabbage Down* is a popular play-party and dance song which, according to Dorothy Scarborough*, was sung before the Civil War. The tune enjoyed widespread popularity throughout the South and was often played for square dances.

### SKIP TO MY LOU

*Skip To My Lou* is one of the best known of all play-party songs. It was one that my great-grandfather Kelley of Knoxville liked to sing to my grandmother when she was a child. Perrow* says that *Lou* is an old Scottish dialect word for sweetheart commonly used in Eastern Tennessee.

### PLAY-PARTY SONGS

Henry Beldon* defines play-party as a "substitute for a dancing party developed in communities where moral or religious taboo has been attached to the word *dance*." Usually the participants of the play-party provided their own music by singing. Certain actions were associated with the words to various play-party songs and they were sung and danced by children as well as young adults.

### HOLY MANNA

I first heard *Holy Manna* from Robert L. Dickey of Memphis. Mr. Dickey remembered this old shape-note hymn as a favorite in his boyhood church in Brookhaven, Mississippi. The Pleasant Grove Baptist Church, which is over 100 years old, formerly used the *Sacred Harp Hymnbook*. The earliest printed source of the hymn is in the *Columbian Harmony*, published in 1825. *Holy Manna* was often sung in the "singing schools" that were common in the South after the Civil War.

### LIZA JANE

Carl Sandburg* said "There are as many 'Liza' songs in the Appalachian Mountains as there are specific trees on the slopes of that range." A text that is very close to the one in this book can be found in Brown's *North Carolina Folklore, vol. 3*.* There are many variations in both black and white folk traditions.

* See Bibliography, p. 103.

*Liza Jane* is a great toe-tapping dance tune.  Find the high note at the 10th fret before you start to play.  Follow the strum guides carefully in measures 3 and 9.

# Liza Jane
*Ionian Mode*

arr. Larkin Bryant

2. You got a gal and I got none, *lil' Liza Jane*;
   Come my love, and be my hon, *lil' Liza Jane*.
   Oh, *lil' Liza, lil' Liza Jane*,
   Oh, *lil' Liza, lil' Liza Jane*.

3. Come my love, and live with me, *lil' Liza Jane*;
   I will take good care of thee, *lil' Liza Jane*.
   Oh, *lil' Liza, lil' Liza Jane*,
   Oh, *lil' Liza, lil' Liza Jane*.

Copyright © 1982 **IVORY PALACES** Music Publishing Company, Inc.  3141 Spottswood Avenue • Memphis, Tennessee • 38111
All rights reserved, including the right to photocopy.

# Liza Jane
## Harmony Part for Second Dulcimer

arr. Larkin Bryant

Copyright © 1982 **IVORY PALACES** Music Publishing Company, Inc. 3141 Spottswood Avenue • Memphis, Tennessee • 38111
All rights reserved, including the right to photocopy.

ENHANCING FAMILIAR TUNES
BY USING SIMPLE PARALLEL CHORDS IN $^D_A A$ TUNING

By using a series of simple two-finger chord positions called parallel chords, you can play harmony and melody at the same time. You'll continue to play the melody on the treble string(s) like you've been doing, and you'll add the harmony by fretting the bass string at the same time.

You'll use different fingerings at times for these chords, but the positions shown below will work for most songs. Be sure to arch your fingers over the fretboard.

Thumb on the treble string(s)
Middle or Index finger on
bass string

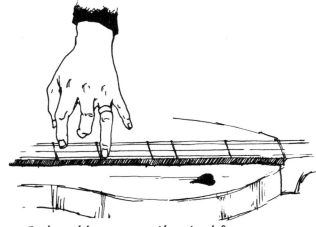

Index finger on the treble
string(s); Ring finger on
bass string

The fret numbers for chord positions are stacked vertically, with the bass string fret numbers on the top line, as shown below. Play all the strings at the same time.

bass string: 1
middle string: 0
treble string(s): 2

To play parallel chords in $^D_A A$ tuning, simply fret the bass string one fret behind the treble string(s). You have to play a slightly different chord position at the 7th and 14th frets to make the harmony sound right. Try out these fret positions as your hand moves up the fretboard.

```
bass string    D  1—2—3—4—5—7—7—8—9—10—11—12—14—14—15—16—
middle string  A  0—0—0—0—0—0—0—0—0— 0— 0— 0—0— 0— 0— 0—
treble string(s)A 2—3—4—5—6—7—8—9—10-11—12—13—14—15—16—17—
```

Take the tunes you've already learned and enrich them with these parallel chords. Here's *Aunt Rhodie* with the chords written out. Be sure to leave your fingers on the strings as you change fret positions.

# Go Tell Aunt Rhodie

*Ionian Mode*

arr. Larkin Bryant

Go      tell Aunt Rho - die,   Go      tell Aunt Rho - die,

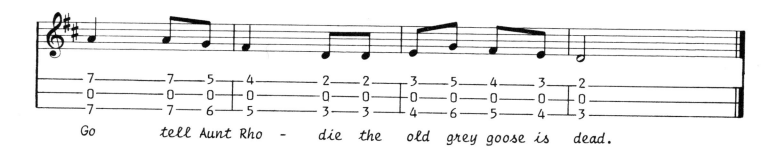

Go      tell Aunt Rho - die the  old  grey goose is  dead.

STRUMMING IN ¾ (WALTZ) TIME

Up to this point, all the tunes have been in $\frac{2}{4}$ time which has 2 beats per measure. $\frac{3}{4}$ time has 3 beats per measure so the basic strum has to be changed slightly to fit the extra beat. The first beat of every measure in $\frac{3}{4}$ time is accented.

Here are some strums that are good to use in $\frac{3}{4}$ time.

1.  - - -   ☐☐  Ex. 16 (Sounds like you're saying, "boom boom boom")
    * * *

2.  - . . . .  ☐☐  Ex. 17 (Sounds like, "boom-chick-a chick-a")
    * * *

3.  - . . -  ☐☐  Ex. 18 (Sounds like, "boom chick-a boom")
    * * *

Copyright © 1982 **IVORY PALACES** Music Publishing Company, Inc. 3141 Spottswood Avenue • Memphis, Tennessee • 38111
All rights reserved, including the right to photocopy.

*Down In The Valley* contains some of the parallel chords listed on the previous page as well as some new chords: $\frac{4}{4}$ and $\frac{1}{0}$. Notice that the tune is in $\frac{3}{4}$ time. ⬤⬤

# Down In The Valley
## Ionian mode

arr. Larkin Bryant

Copyright © 1982 **IVORY PALACES** Music Publishing Company, Inc. 3141 Spottswood Avenue • Memphis, Tennessee • 38111

All rights reserved, including the right to photocopy.

o - ver, hear the wind blow.

2. Write me a letter, send it by mail,
   Send it in care of the Birmingham jail;
   Birmingham jail, love, Birmingham jail,
   Send it in care of the Birmingham jail.

3. If you don't love me, love whom you please,
   Throw your arms 'round me, give my heart ease;
   Give my heart ease, dear, give my heart ease,
   Throw your arms 'round me, give your heart ease.

4. Roses love sunshine, violets love dew,
   Angels in heaven know I love you;
   Know I love you, dear, know I love you,
   Angels in heaven know I love you.

NEW CHORDS IN D/A/A TUNING

The new chords in each tuning will be listed as they appear in the songs.

| D  CHORDS | | | A  CHORDS | | | A7  CHORD |
|---|---|---|---|---|---|---|
| 2 | 4 | 7ᴵ | 1 | 1 | 4 | 3 |
| 0 | 0 | 0 | 0 | 0 | 0 | 0 |
| 3 | 5 | 7ᵀ | 0 | 2 | 4 | 4 |

## MORE EASY PARALLEL CHORDS IN $\begin{smallmatrix}D\\A\\A\end{smallmatrix}$ TUNING

Here is another easy way to play parallel chords in $\begin{smallmatrix}D\\A\\A\end{smallmatrix}$ tuning. This time the harmony is played on the middle string while the melody is played on the treble string(s). Suggested fingerings are thumb or index finger on the treble string(s) and middle or ring finger on the middle string. The fret numbers for chord positions are stacked vertically with the bass string fret number on top.

```
bass string      D —0— 0— 0— 0— 0— 0— 0— 0—— 0—— 0—— 0—— 0—— 0—— 0-
middle string    A —0— 2— 3— 4— 5— 6— 7— 8—— 9——10——11——12——13——14·
treble string(s) A —3— 4— 5— 6— 7— 8— 9——10——11——12——13——14——15——16-
```

Notice that the middle string is usually played two frets behind the treble string(s) with the exception of the 3rd fret which sounds better played with the open middle and bass strings. Leave out the 6½ fret if you have it. Try playing some songs you already know with these parallel chords.

## FILLS

Some songs like *Wildwood Flower* have long notes at the end of some of the musical phrases. You can fill in these long holds with extra notes to make the song more interesting. Fills are put in the tablature but not in the music notation since they aren't part of the melody. Watch for them since they are found at the end of songs as well as between phrases.

## PLAYING MELODY WHILE HOLDING DOWN A CHORD

In the last few songs, you've changed chord positions for every melody note. Sometimes, you have to hold down one chord position while you play several melody notes. A very simple example of this is found in *Wildwood Flower* in measure 3. The fret numbers for the treble string(s) are 4-5-4 but you play them while holding the $\begin{smallmatrix}4\\0\\4\end{smallmatrix}$ chord position.

```
— 4 I(M)— 4 ——— 4 —
— 0 ——— 0 ——— 0 —
— 4 R —— 5 T ——4 R —
```

A few strategically placed chords add a lot of spice without bogging you down in a fast tune.  Once you've learned what's written here, however, feel free to add as many chords as you like for variety.  Measures 13 and 14 contain some of the new parallel chords you've just learned.  Look carefully at the strum guides for measures 15 and 16. □□

# Wildwood Flower

Ionian Mode

arr. Larkin Bryant

Copyright © 1982 **IVORY PALACES** Music Publishing Company, Inc.  3141 Spottswood Avenue • Memphis, Tennessee • 38111
All rights reserved, including the right to photocopy.

2.  I'll think of him never, I'll be wildly gay,
    I'll charm every heart and the crowd I will sway.
    I'll live yet to see him regret the dark hour,
    When he won then neglected the frail wildwood flower.

3.  He told me he loved me and promised to love,
    Through ill and misfortune, all others above.
    Another has won him, Oh! misery to tell,
    He left me in silence no words of farewell!

4.  He taught me to love him, he called me his flower,
    That blossom'd for him all the brighter each hour.
    But I woke from my dreaming, my idol was clay,
    My visions of love have all faded away.

NEW CHORDS IN D A A TUNING

D CHORD

  0
  5
  7

G CHORDS

0   0
6   6 R
8   10 T

Sweet Hour of Prayer uses a combination of both types of $^D_A$A parallel chords.
Play the tune at a moderate speed like a waltz.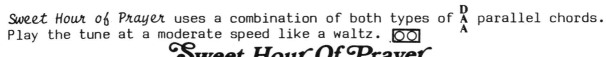

Copyright © 1982 IVORY PALACES Music Publishing Company, Inc. 3141 Spottswood Avenue • Memphis, Tennessee • 38111
All rights reserved, including the right to photocopy.

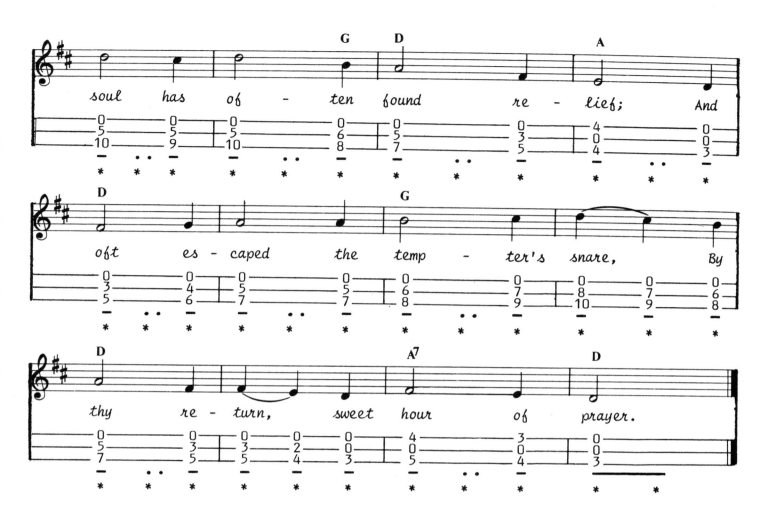

NEW CHORDS IN D A A TUNING

D CHORDS

0   0
3   5 R
5   10 T

G CHORD

0
8
10

## HISTORICAL NOTES

### DOWN IN THE VALLEY

Jean Thomas* states that this song is the "best loved of the lonesome tunes of the Kentucky mountains." Though commonly associated with the Anglo-American tradition, the song was occasionally sung by black folksingers.

### WILDWOOD FLOWER

*Wildwood Flower* is an example of a popular parlor song which was originally circulated by sheet music or in songbooks and later went into oral tradition. The original song, entitled *I'll Twine 'Mid the Ringlets* was composed by Maud Irving and J.D. Webster and published in 1860. By the early 1900's it had passed into folk tradition with many variations in the text.

### SWEET HOUR OF PRAYER

The text to this beautiful old hymn was first printed in *The New York Observer* in 1845. According to the Rev.T.Salmon, who sent *The Observer* the text, the hymn was written by a blind preacher, Rev.W.W.Walford, in Warwickshire, England. Later research indicated that a Rev.Walford did not fit Salmon's description, and thus the author of the text remains somewhat of a mystery. The tune, however, was composed especially for the hymn by Bradbury, who first published it in his collection, *Golden Chain*, 1861.

### HEY!HO! NOBODY HOME

*Hey!Ho!* appears in *Pammelia*, the earliest English printed collection of rounds and catches, edited by Thomas Ravenscroft and printed in 1609. It is a catch, which is a type of round or canon written for three or more male voices. Catches were known for their sportive words and were popular among the working class men rather than the gentry. The words printed in *Pammelia* are as follows: "Hey ho, nobody at home; meat nor drink nor money have I none; fill the pot, Eddy." The tune is anonymous.

### SCARBOROUGH FAIR (THE ELFIN KNIGHT) - *Child Ballad No.2*

According to Francis Child,* the earliest known source of this ballad is a Scottish broadside entitled A *Discourse Betwixt A Young Woman and The Elfin Knight*, Edinborough, about 1670. The riddle theme, a contest of wits, is prevalent in folk tales and songs all over the world.

* See Bibliography, p. 103.

## THE DORIAN MODE

The Dorian mode is a minor sounding mode. It has a beautiful, haunting quality. The Dorian mode begins at the 4th fret and continues (leaving out the 6½ fret) up to the 11th fret.

### DORIAN MODE

| *The RE scale* | re | mi | fa | sol | la | ti | do | re |
|---|---|---|---|---|---|---|---|---|
| *Frets* | 4 | 5 | 6 | 7 | 8 | 9 | 10 | 11 |
| *Note names for D Dorian scale* | D | E | F | G | A | B | C | D |

Here is the traditional way to tune the dulcimer to play tunes with a Dorian melody:

TUNING TO **D** *bass string*
**A** *middle string*
**G** *treble string(s)*

Ex.19 *If you're already tuned to* $_A^D$*, go to step 3.*

1. Tune the bass string to low D. If you want to tune the dulcimer to itself, pick a note at random and follow the next steps.
2. Fret the bass string at the 4th fret and tune the open middle string to sound the same as the fretted bass string.
3. Now, fret the bass string at the 3rd fret and tune the open treble string(s) to sound the same as the fretted bass string.

You're tuned to these notes:

On the piano:

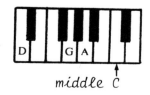

*middle C*

On the guitar:

 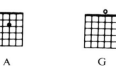

D          A          G

## ROUNDS

Rounds were a popular form of entertainment during the reign of Elizabeth I in sixteenth century England. The earliest known round, *Summer Is Icumen In,* dates from about 1310. As the name implies, a round goes in a circle with three or four voices following each other, singing the same melody at the same pitch.

*Hey! Ho! Nobody Home* is a round for 3 dulcimers or three groups of dulcimers.

DULCIMER I      starts at the beginning and plays the song 3 or more times, adding the ending measure the last time through.

DULCIMER II     starts at the beginning when dulcimer I reaches ② and plays the song 3 or more times, adding the ending measure the last time through.

DULCIMER III    starts at the beginning when dulcimer I reaches ③ and plays the song 3 or more times, adding the ending measure the last time through.

*Hey! Ho! Nobody Home* is written out like the earlier songs since it has no chords. Look carefully at the strum guides for measure 5 which has dotted notes. Notice the fast melody notes in measure 6 that are played with *L/R* strums. Measure 6 also requires some finger dexterity, and here are some fingering suggestions:

8T   7I   6R   5R   or   8T   7I   6T   5I   or   8T   7I   6M   5R

# Hey! Ho! Nobody Home

*Dorian Mode*

arr. Larkin Bryant

DAG tuning

Hey Ho, no-bo-dy home; meat nor drink nor money have I none.

Still I will be ve - ry merry merry.

ending

Copyright © 1982 **IVORY PALACES** Music Publishing Company, Inc. 3141 Spottswood Avenue • Memphis, Tennessee • 38111
All rights reserved, including the right to photocopy.

42

# Part II: Intermediate Techniques

## FINGERPICKING

When you use your fingers instead of a pick to strike the strings, you are fingerpicking.  I like to use three fingers to pluck the strings:

middle finger on the bass string ———————————

index finger on the middle string ———————————

thumb on the treble string(s) ———————————

These fingers will consistently pluck the same strings.  The index and middle fingers pluck the strings in toward yourself while the thumb plucks the treble string(s) out away from yourself.

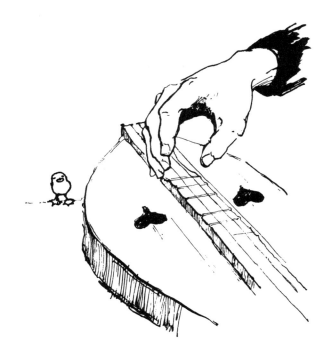

Brace the little finger against the side of the fingerboard or rest it on top of the dulcimer to keep your hand in the right place for picking.

Arch your fingers over the strings so that each finger is above the string it plucks.

## FOLKSTYLE FINGERPICKING

Folkstyle fingerpicking is a very smooth, constantly flowing style. Its even rhythm patterns make it a good choice for new fingerpickers. Here are some picking patterns for songs in $\frac{3}{4}$ time. *These patterns can be played in any tuning.* However, they are demonstrated in $\begin{smallmatrix}D\\A\\G\end{smallmatrix}$ tuning on the companion tape.

## READING FINGERPICKING TABLATURE

The horizontal lines represent the dulcimer strings. Double treble strings are shown as a single line. Read the fingerpicking tablature from left to right like the strumming tablature but pluck only one string at a time. Be sure to practice each pattern several times.

Picking Pattern No.1 in $\frac{3}{4}$ time: 🔳 Ex.20

Pluck the strings one at a time in the following order. Use all open (0) strings for now.

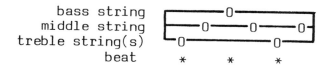

Picking Pattern No.2 in $\frac{3}{4}$ time: 🔳 Ex.21

In this pattern the treble and middle strings are plucked alternately.

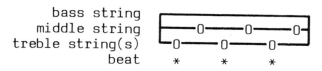

Variation on
Picking Pattern No.2 in $\frac{3}{4}$ time: 🔳 Ex.22

In this pattern the treble and bass strings are plucked alternately.

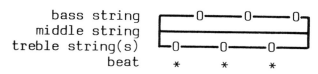

## FINGERPICKING EXERCISES

Now that you've had a chance to try some picking patterns on open strings, here are the same patterns with fret numbers on the treble string(s).

1. The first exercise uses picking pattern No.1 in $\frac{3}{4}$ time going part way up the Dorian scale (tune to $\begin{smallmatrix}D\\A\\G\end{smallmatrix}$). See if you can go the rest of the way up the scale on your own. Listen to the companion tape if you're not sure how it should go. Play the exercises slowly and evenly.

Ex.23    bass string
         middle string
         treble string(s)
         beat

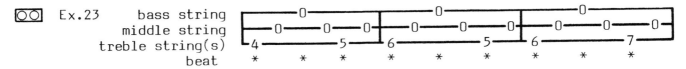

2. The second exercise uses picking pattern No. 2 and goes up the Dorian scale in a round about way. See if you can complete this exercise on your own.

Ex.24    bass string
         middle string
         treble string(s)
         beat

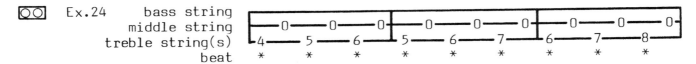

3. Do exercise 2, plucking the bass string instead of the middle string.

In doing these exercises, you've seen how the melody can be played on the treble string(s) with the other strings played open as in traditional mountain strumming style. The first fingerpicking tunes are arranged in this manner.

## MUSICAL REPEAT SYMBOLS

When you see numbered brackets over the final measures, play the first bracketed measure and go back to the beginning as often as desired or for the number of verses indicated (1,2). The last time through the song, skip the first bracketed measure and play the second bracketed measure .

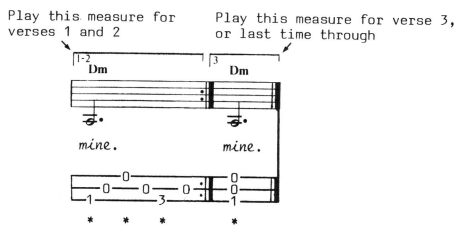

Play this measure for verses 1 and 2

Play this measure for verse 3, or last time through

Sometimes, you are to repeat a song from a starting point other than the beginning as in *Scarborough Fair*. In *Lord Lovel*, for example, you play the song from the beginning to the repeat marks :‖ at the end of the first bracketed measure, then go back to the repeat marks ‖: near the beginning of the song. Play the song as many times as you like from the beginning repeat marks to the final repeat marks. The last time through the song, skip the first bracketed measure and play the second bracketed measure.

## THE BRUSH TECHNIQUE

When you see fret numbers stacked vertically in fingerpicking tablature $\begin{smallmatrix}0\\0\\4\end{smallmatrix}$, you can play all the notes at once by using your thumb as a pick, brushing across all the strings from treble string(s) to bass.

Ex.25
```
— 0 —
— 0 —
— 4 —
```

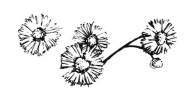

The arrangement for *Scarborough Fair* is made up of fingerpicking patterns No. 1 and No. 2. The melody is entirely on the treble string(s). You can go over the treble string(s) fret numbers by themselves or strum them to get familiar with the tune before tackling the picking patterns. Play the song slowly and evenly. 🔲🔲

Copyright © 1982 **IVORY PALACES** Music Publishing Company, Inc. 3141 Spottswood Avenue • Memphis, Tennessee • 38111
All rights reserved, including the right to photocopy.

The duet part to *Scarborough Fair* is really lovely and I encourage you to find a playing partner to share this song with you. Also, you can sing the melody while playing the duet part on the dulcimer.

# Scarborough Fair
Harmony Part for Second Dulcimer

arr. Larkin Bryant

D A G tuning

1. Are you going to Scar - bor - ough Fair? Pars - ley, sage, rose - ma - ry and thyme; Re-mem - ber me to one who lives there, For she once was a true love of mine. mine.

2. Tell her to make me a cambric shirt:
Parsley, sage, rosemary and thyme;
Without no seams nor fancy work,
Then she'll be a true love of mine.

3. Tell her to find me an acre of land:
Parsley, sage, rosemary and thyme;
Between the salt water and the sea strand;
Then she'll be a true love of mine.

Copyright © 1982 **IVORY PALACES** Music Publishing Company, Inc. 3141 Spottswood Avenue • Memphis, Tennessee • 38111<br>All rights reserved, including the right to photocopy.

50

While you're in $\begin{smallmatrix}D\\A\\G\end{smallmatrix}$, here's a strumming tune with chords. The main idea here is holding down part of a chord (in this case $\begin{smallmatrix}6\\0\end{smallmatrix}$ or $\begin{smallmatrix}7\\0\end{smallmatrix}$ on the bass and middle string) while you play the melody on the treble string(s). To do this easily requires careful fingering and I have made some suggestions in the tablature. Other techniques to watch out for are fills and fast notes (measures 1 and 5). [OO]

# Pretty Polly
*Dorian Mode*

arr. Larkin Bryant

$\begin{smallmatrix}D\\A\\G\end{smallmatrix}$ tuning

CHORDS IN $\begin{smallmatrix}D\\A\\G\end{smallmatrix}$

| Dm CHORDS | | | F CHORD |
|---|---|---|---|
| 0 | 4 | 7 | 6 |
| 0 | 0 | 0 | 0 |
| 4 | 4 | 9 | 6 |

Copyright © 1982 **IVORY PALACES** Music Publishing Company, Inc. • 3141 Spottswood Avenue • Memphis, Tennessee • 38111
All rights reserved, including the right to photocopy.

1. Polly, pretty Polly, come go along with me,
   Polly, pretty Polly, come go along with me,
   Before we get married some pleasure to see.

2. My mind is to marry and never to part,
   My mind is to marry and never to part,
   The first time I saw her it wounded my heart.

3. He led her over mountains and valleys so deep,
   He led her over mountains and valleys so deep,
   Pretty Polly mistrusted and then began to weep.

4. Willie, little Willie, I'm afraid of your ways,
   Willie, little Willie, I'm afraid of your ways,
   The way you've been rambling, you'll lead me astray.

5. Polly, pretty Polly, you're guessing 'bout right,
   Polly, pretty Polly, you're guessing 'bout right,
   I dug on your grave for the best part of last night.

6. He stabbed her to the heart and her heart's blood did flow,
   He stabbed her to the heart and her heart's blood did flow,
   And into the grave pretty Polly did go.

7. He threw the dirt over her and turned away to go,
   He threw the dirt over her and turned away to go,
   Down to the river where the deep waters flow.

## EMBELLISHING TUNES WITH
## FANCY FINGER TECHNIQUES FOR THE FRETTING HAND

The following finger techniques, borrowed from guitar and banjo playing, can be incorporated into any tune to embellish it. With a little practice they're easy to do, and they add a lot of *pizazz* to your playing.

The following techniques are demonstrated in $\begin{smallmatrix}D\\A\\G\end{smallmatrix}$ on the tape.

### HAMMERED NOTES ⓗ

Hammering notes is a fancy way to go from an open string to a fretted note, or from a fretted note to a higher fretted note.

### HAMMERING FROM AN OPEN STRING TO A FRETTED NOTE

For example, say that you want to hammer from 0 to 1 on the treble string(s). The tablature would be written like this:  0 ⓗ 1.  ⬚⬚  Ex.26

1. Pluck the open treble string(s) with the picking hand.
2. With the string(s) still ringing, raise the left index finger high above the 1st fret and *QUICKLY and FIRMLY* "hammer" onto the 1st fret causing the string to sound without being plucked. The finger motion should be like a hammer hitting a nail. Listen to the companion tape to hear how it should sound. Any finger or fret can be used for hammering. Practice with the ring and middle fingers once you have gotten the technique with the index finger. You must use lots of force to get the note to sound by itself.

### HAMMERING FROM A FRETTED NOTE TO A HIGHER FRETTED NOTE

You can also hammer from a fretted note to a higher fretted note, for example from the 3rd fret to the 4th fret on the treble string(s). The tablature would be written like this:  3 ⓗ 4.  ⬚⬚  Ex.27

1. Fret the 3rd fret on the treble string(s) with the ring finger. *LEAVE THE RING FINGER IN POSITION* on the 3rd fret and arch the index finger or thumb over the 4th fret. Pluck the treble string(s) with the picking hand.

2. Leaving the ring finger in position at the 3rd fret, and with the string(s) still ringing, *QUICKLY and FIRMLY* "hammer" the index finger or thumb onto the 4th fret, causing the note at that fret to sound without being plucked.

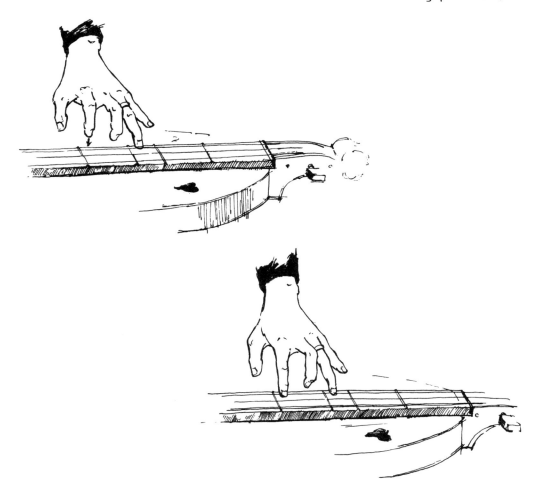

## HAMMERING AND STRUMMING

Hammering techniques are the same in strumming songs, except that you strum all the strings first, and then "hammer" the indicated note by itself.  In strum tablature hammering on from the open treble string(s) to the 1st fret would look like this: ▢ Ex.28

```
——— 0 ————————
——— 0 ————
——— 0   h  ①—
```

Hammering from the 3rd fret to the 4th fret in strumming tablature would look like this: ▢ Ex.29

```
——— 0 ———————
——— 0 ————
——— 3 (h) 4 —
```

PULL OFFS  ⓟ

A pull off is the opposite of a hammer on.  It goes from a fretted note to an open string or from a fretted note to a lower fretted note.

### PULLING OFF FROM A FRETTED NOTE TO AN OPEN STRING

An example would be pulling off from the 1st fret on the treble string(s) to the open treble string(s).  It would look like this in the tablature: 1 ⓟ 0.

⊡ Ex.30

1. Fret the treble string(s) at the 1st fret with the index finger and pluck the string(s) with the picking hand.

2. With the string(s) still ringing and with the index finger at the 1st fret, press down and pull off the string toward you, causing the open string(s) to sound.  This technique takes a little practice to get right. Listen to the companion tape to hear how it should sound.  A pull off can be done with any finger from any fret.  Try using the ring finger and thumb to do pull offs.

### PULLING OFF FROM A FRETTED NOTE TO A LOWER FRETTED NOTE

For example, try pulling off from the 4th fret to the 3rd fret on the treble string(s).  It would look like this in the tablature:  4 ⓟ 3.  ⊡  Ex.31

1. Fret *both* the 4th fret (use index finger or thumb) and the 3rd fret (use the ring finger) on the treble string(s) and pluck the string(s) with the picking hand.

2. With the string(s) still ringing, and with the ring finger remaining at
   the 3rd fret, press down and pull off the index finger or thumb from the
   4th fret.  This will cause the third fret note to sound.

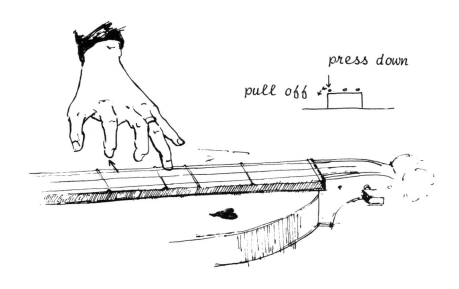

### STRUMMING AND PULLING OFF

   Pulling off techniques are the same in strumming as in fingerpicking.  The
difference is that you strum all the strings first and then pull off the indicated
note.  Pulling off from the first fret to an open string looks like this in
strumming tablature: 〔OO〕 Ex.32

```
——— 0 ———————
——— 0 ———————
——— 1 ⓟ 0 ——
     ‾
strum pull off to 0
```

Pulling off from the fourth fret to the third fret would look like this: 〔OO〕 Ex.33

```
——— 0 ———————
——— 0 ———————
——— 4 ⓟ 3 ——
     ‾
strum pull off to 3
```

## SLIDES ⌣

A slide uses the same finger to go from one fret to another fret.  You can use any finger or thumb to do a slide.  As an example, slide from the 3rd fret to the 4th fret with the index finger.  It would look like this in the tablature: 3⌣4.

[OO] Ex.34

1. Fret the treble string(s) with the index finger at the 3rd fret and pluck the string(s) with the picking hand.
2. With the string(s) still ringing, slide the index finger to the 4th fret, causing it to sound without re-plucking the string.

Try sliding up and down the scale in the places indicated: [OO] Ex.35

3  4  5⌣6  7  8  9⌣10  10  9  8⌣7  6  5  4⌣3

## HARMONICS °

Harmonics are bell-like tones that can be played at certain frets on the dulcimer.  The easiest harmonics are at the 7th and 14th frets, but you can also get them at the 4th, 11th and 3rd frets on any string.

1. To make a harmonic, lightly touch the string *directly OVER the fret.* Do not press down the string like you do for normal fretting.
2. Pluck the string with the picking hand.
3. Immediately lift the fretting finger off the string(s) so that the string(s) can vibrate freely.  As an example, try the 7th fret with the index finger on the treble string(s).

[OO] Ex.36  7°

57

## THE AEOLIAN MODE

The Aeolian mode sounds like a minor scale. It has a sad, mournful quality. The Aeolian mode begins at the 1st fret and continues (leaving out the 6½ fret) up to the 8th fret.

### AEOLIAN MODE

| | | | | | | | | |
|---|---|---|---|---|---|---|---|---|
| *The LA scale* | la | ti | do | re | mi | fa | sol | la |
| *Frets* | 1 | 2 | 3 | 4 | 5 | 6 | 7 | 8 |
| *Note names for D Aeolian scale* | D | E | F | G | A | B♭ | C | D |

D Aeolian tunes may be accompanied in the key of Dm (D minor) by other instruments. Here is the traditional way to tune the dulcimer to play tunes with an Aeolian melody in D:

**TUNING TO**  **D** *bass string*
**A** *middle string*
**C** *treble string(s)*

 Ex.37

1. Tune the bass string to low D, or pick a random note and tune the dulcimer to itself following the next two steps.

2. Fret the bass string at the 4th fret and tune the open middle string to sound the same as the fretted bass string.

3. Now, fret the bass string at the 6th fret and tune the open treble string(s) to sound the same as the fretted bass string. You'll be tuning the treble strings higher than you did for $\begin{smallmatrix}D\\A\\A\end{smallmatrix}$ and $\begin{smallmatrix}D\\A\\G\end{smallmatrix}$.

You're tuned to these notes:

On the piano:

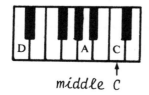

*middle C*

On the guitar:

58

Lord Lovel uses fingerpicking patterns No.1 and No.2 with the melody on the treble string(s) like Scarborough Fair. This arrangement has the added finger techniques of hammered notes, slides and pull offs. Listen to the tape to hear how the hammered notes and pull offs are played in rhythm with the tune. ⬚⬚

# Lord Lovel
## Aeolian Mode

arr. Larkin Bryant

Copyright © 1982 IVORY PALACES Music Publishing Company, Inc. 3141 Spottswood Avenue • Memphis, Tennessee • 38111
All rights reserved, including the right to photocopy.

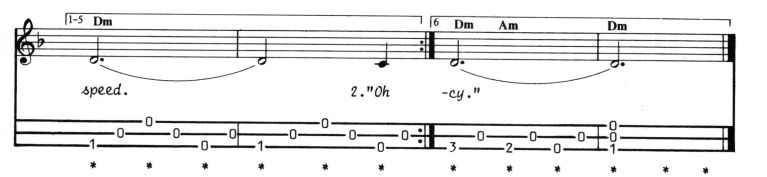

1. Lord Lovel he stood at his castle gate,
   A-combing his milk-white steed;
   When up came Lady Nancy Belle,
   To wish her lover good speed, good speed,
   To wish her lover good speed.

2. "Oh, where are you going, Lord Lovel?" she said,
   "Oh, where are going?" said she;
   "I'm going, my Lady Nancy Belle,
   Strange countries for to see, to see,
   Strange countries for to see."

3. "When will you be back, Lord Lovel?" she said,
   "Oh, when will you come back?" said she;
   "In a year or two, or three, at the most,
   I'll return to my fair Nancy, Nancy,
   I'll return to my fair Nancy."

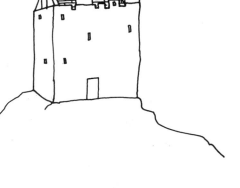

4. But he had not been gone a year and a day,
   Strange countries for to see;
   When languishing thoughts came into his head,
   Lady Nancy Belle he would go see, go see,
   Lady Nancy Belle he would go see.

5. So he rode, and he rode, on his milk-white steed,
   Till he came to London town;
   And there he heard St. Pancras bells,
   And the people all mourning round, around,
   And the people all mourning round.

6. "Oh, what's the matter?" Lord Lovel he said,
   "Oh, what's the matter?" said he;
   "A lord's lady is dead" a woman replied,
   "And some call her Lady Nancy, Nancy,
   And some call her Lady Nancy."

## HISTORICAL NOTES

### BROADSIDE BALLAD

The term *broadside ballad* refers to a narrative song which was printed on cheap paper and sold in the streets of England in the 17-19th centuries. Many of these songs eventually entered into oral tradition and became popular folk songs in England and America.

### PRETTY POLLY

As ballads are passed down through oral tradition, portions are lost or changed often to adapt the story to local occurrences. *Pretty Polly* is a shortened version of a long British ballad that dates from the mid-18th century, called *The Gaspard Tragedy*. Cox* reports a West Virginia version which has reference to a Polly Alderidge who was murdered by William Chapman near Warfield, Ky. about 1820.

### LORD LOVEL - *Child Ballad No.75*

*Lord Lovel* was probably the most popular Child ballad in America during the mid-1800's. Henry Beldon* states that practically all American texts relate to a London broadside of 1846 (Child H). Its popularity is proven by the fact that it was parodied during the Civil War for political purposes. *The New Battle of Lord Lovel* was a parody about Mansfield Lovell, a confederate officer who failed to defend New Orleans against Farragut in 1862. The ballad was also parodied to satirize Lincoln. I first heard *Lord Lovel* played on the dulcimer by Jean Simmons of Mountain View, Arkansas.

### SHADY GROVE

This popular song and dance tune has many variations, often consisting of various floating verses. The tune may derive its name from the towns of Shady Grove, Kentucky or Virginia.

* See Bibliography, p. 103.

Shady Grove is easy to play once you get the hang of doing the hammered notes and pull offs. Practice the first measure over and over by itself until you get the lilt of the rhythm. Be sure to listen to the companion tape. Shady Grove has only 5 notes in the melody. It can be played in D A G tuning (with different fret numbers) as well as D A C. ☐☐

# Shady Grove
## Aeolian Mode

1. Peaches in the summertime,
Apples in the fall,
If I can't have the girl I love,
Won't have none at all.

2. If I had a needle and thread,
Fine as I could sew,
I'd sew my gal to my coat tails,
And down the road we'd go.

3. Higher up on the cherry trees,
The riper grow the cherries,
The more you kiss and hug the girls,
The more they want to marry.

Copyright © 1982 IVORY PALACES Music Publishing Company, Inc. 3141 Spottswood Avenue • Memphis, Tennessee • 38111
All rights reserved, including the right to photocopy.

## HISTORICAL NOTES

### MARY HAMILTON (FOUR MARYS) - Child Ballad No. 173

This is a Scottish ballad which Francis Child* states as appearing around 1719-1764. It is not a popular ballad in America. The tale seems to be a mixture of two similar historical incidents: one in the court of Mary, Queen of Scots in 1563; the other in the court of Czar Peter of Russia in 1718.

There were four Marys who attended Queen Mary of Scotland, but their last names were Fleming, Livingston, Seton and Beaton. However, a French woman who served in the Queen's chamber had a child by the Queen's apothecary. The maidservant murdered the child and both she and the apothecary were hanged in Edinborough.

Mary Hambleton, a young Scottish lady who was a maid of honor to the Empress Catherine, murdered several children that she had by the Czar's aide-de-camp. One of the children was reported to have been found at the bottom of a well wrapped in a court napkin. On the day of her execution, she dressed up in white silk with black ribbons in an effort to touch Czar Peter's heart. She begged for mercy. He refused her and Mary was beheaded.

### SHENANDOAH

Variations of this folksong have been sung by sailormen, rivermen and armymen. Alan Lomax* suggests that the origin of the song might come from American or Canadian voyageurs. Many American folksongs of the sea may be of Afro-American origin; Maud Cuney-Hare* says that "one of the best windlass songs of the Negro is Shanadore." A variation of Shanadore was sung by the regular army, according to Carl Sandburg,* in 1897. John and Alan Lomax* note that the cavalry sang a version of their own called The Wild Mizzourrye.

### OLD JOE CLARK

Old Joe Clark is a popular play-party and dance song in both white and black traditions. One square dance caller said that he knew one hundred and forty-four verses to the tune. The true identity of Joe Clark remains a mystery, though some sources claim him to be a Virginia moonshiner.

* See Bibliography, p. 103.

## USING CHORDS WITH FINGERPICKING

The way you chord a fingerpicked tune is no different from the way you chord a strummed tune. It is the picking hand that changes, from strumming all the strings at once to plucking individual strings. In other words, you could finger-pick any of the songs in the strumming tablature by changing the strumming patterns to fingerpicking patterns.

Chords do look different in fingerpicking tablature because they're stretched out instead of being neatly stacked. If you know your chord positions well you'll recognize them even in this "toppled over" condition! Here are some common chords in $\frac{D}{A}_{A}$ tuning in both tablatures.

STRUMMING TABLATURE          FINGERPICKING TABLATURE

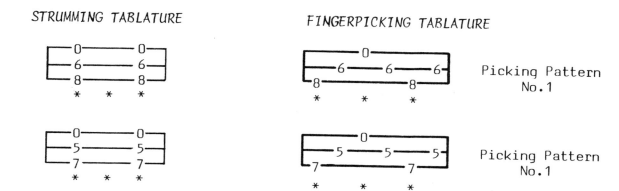

Remember that often the melody changes from a chord position:

Often chords change in the middle of a measure, like this:

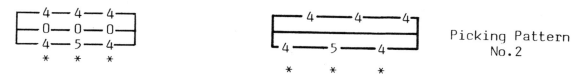

If you have trouble recognizing chord positions, try circling them with a pencil like this:

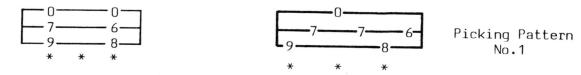

Mary Hamilton uses chords with Picking Patterns No.1 and No.2. Most of the chords have been used in other D A A songs and should be familiar. 

# Mary Hamilton
### Ionian Mode

arr. Larkin Bryant

Copyright © 1982 IVORY PALACES Music Publishing Company, Inc. 3141 Spottswood Avenue • Memphis, Tennessee • 38111
All rights reserved, including the right to photocopy.

65

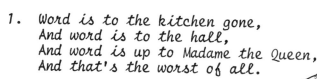

1. Word *is* to the kitchen gone,
   And word *is* to the hall,
   And word *is* up to Madame the Queen,
   And *that's* the worst of all.

2. 'O *rise*, O *rise*, Mary Hamilton,
   O *rise* and tell to me,
   What hast thou done with thy sweet babe,
   I saw and heard weep by thee.'

3. 'I put him in a handkerchief,
   And cast him out to sea,
   And I bade him sink or he might swim,
   He should ne'er come home to me.'

4. 'O *rise*, O *rise*, Mary Hamilton,
   O *rise* and go with me,
   There is a wedding in Glasgow town,
   This day we'll go and see.'

5. As they came into Edinburgh town,
   The city for to see,
   The balie's wife and the provost's wife,
   Said, O and alas for thee!

6. 'Last eve the queen had four Marys,
   This night she'll have but three,
   She had Mary Seaton, and Mary Beaton,
   And Mary Carmichael, and me.'

7. 'Last eve I washed the Queen Mary's feet,
   And bore her to her bed,
   This day she's given me my reward,
   This gallows-tree to tread.'

# HISTORICAL NOTES

## HARRISON TOWN

*Harrison Town* is an obscure outlaw ballad. Two sources were collected by Randolph* in Arkansas, one from a Fayetteville man who learned it around 1905. The tune, which I first heard from the Copeland kids of Mountain View, Arkansas, is particularly beautiful on the dulcimer.

## CRIPPLE CREEK

*Cripple Creek* is one of the most popular of all the American dance tunes. It has strong currency throughout the South and other rural areas in the United States where it is often used for square dancing. The name "Cripple Creek" may come from a well-known mining town area in Virginia.

## DOWN CAME AN ANGEL  (CHRIST WAS BORN IN BETHLEHEM)

*Down Came An Angel* is a lovely, poignant Easter ballad. Sources have been found in West Virginia, North Carolina and Kentucky. Jean Ritchie* met a lady in New York who said she remembered a variation of the song being sung by miners' wives in her native home of Wigan, England. *Christ Was Born In Bethlehem* can be found in *Songs of Gladness*, printed in 1869.

## AMAZING GRACE

There is a powerful and moving story behind the man who wrote one of the best loved hymns in the English language. John Newton, born in England in 1725, was a complete rake in his early years. He was a deserter from the Royal Navy and the captain of a slave ship. His crew mutinied and Newton was put to shore on an island off the coast of Africa. He became, for all practical purposes, a slave himself, working on a fruit plantation for a black woman. Before he was rescued, he almost starved. On the way back to England, the ship was nearly lost during a terrible storm. Newton and the other sailors worked feverishly through the night pumping water out of the ship. When told it was hopeless, Newton cried, "If this will not do, the Lord have mercy on us!" The ship survived. Newton later became a minister and wrote a collection of hymns, one of which was *Amazing Grace*. The hymn, however, did not become a favorite until the text was put to an anonymous American folk tune. *Amazing Grace* was first printed in America in the *Virginia Harmony*, 1831.

* See Bibliography, p. 103.

## FOLKSTYLE FINGERPICKING IN $\frac{4}{4}$ TIME

$\frac{4}{4}$ time has four beats per measure.  The picking patterns are similar to picking patterns in $\frac{3}{4}$ time.  Listen to the companion tape to hear how these patterns sound.  In the following examples one measure of $\frac{4}{4}$ time is shown.

Picking Pattern No.1 in $\frac{4}{4}$ time:  ⊙⊙  Ex.38  (Examples on tape in $\begin{smallmatrix}D\\A\\A\end{smallmatrix}$ tuning.)
    In this pattern the strings are plucked one at a time as indicated.

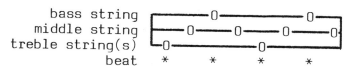

Picking Pattern No.2 in $\frac{4}{4}$ time:  ⊙⊙   Ex.39

    In this pattern the bass string is not plucked.

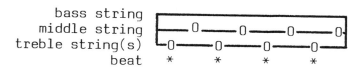

Combination of Picking Patterns No.1 and No.2 in $\frac{4}{4}$ time:  ⊙⊙   Ex.40
    Strings are plucked one at a time in this pattern.

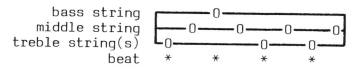

Picking Pattern Variations for Dotted Notes ( ♩.♪ ) in $\frac{4}{4}$ time.
    Strings are plucked one at a time.

⊙⊙    Ex.41                                    ⊙⊙    Ex.42

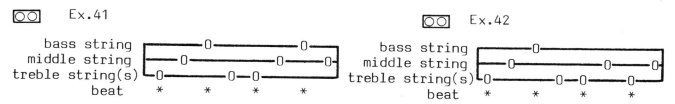

There are lots of other picking patterns that you can do that aren't listed in this book.

*Shenandoah* is a good song for fingerpicking in $\frac{4}{4}$ time. This arrangement uses picking patterns on the previous page. Watch for the three finger chord position in measures 11 and 12.

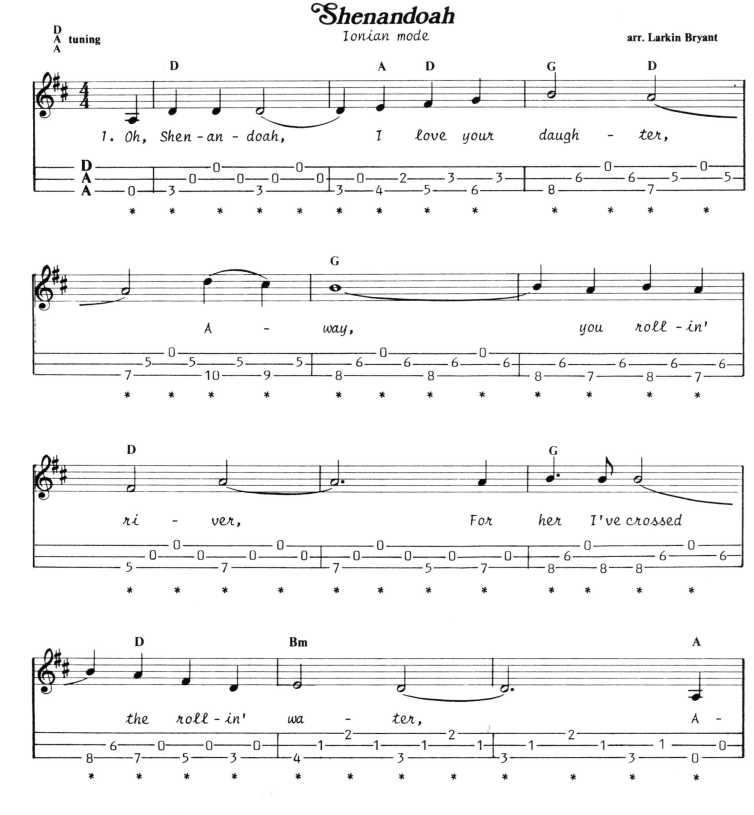

Copyright © 1982 **IVORY PALACES** Music Publishing Company, Inc. 3141 Spottswood Avenue • Memphis, Tennessee • 38111
All rights reserved, including the right to photocopy.

way, we're bound a - way, A -

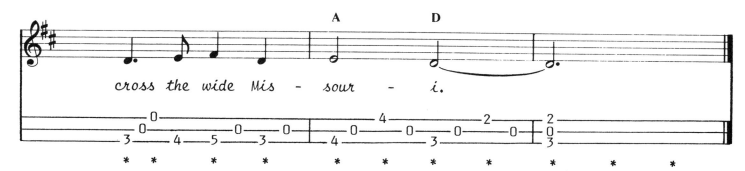

cross the wide Mis - sour - i.

2. The trader loved an Indian maiden,
   Away, you rolling river,
   With presents his canoe was laden,
   Away, I'm bound away,
   Across the wide Missouri.

3. Oh, Shenandoah, I long to hear you,
   Away, you rolling river,
   Oh, Shenandoah, I long to hear you,
   Away, I'm bound away,
   Across the wide Missouri.

NEW
D
A CHORD
A

Bm CHORD
2 I
1 L
3 T

## THE MIXOLYDIAN MODE

The Mixolydian mode sounds the same as the Ionian mode until you get to the seventh tone of the scale which is lowered a half step. It is a very beautiful mode. The scale begins at the open treble string(s) and continues (leaving out the 6½ fret) up to the 7th fret.

### MIXOLYDIAN MODE

| *The SOL scale* | sol | la | ti | do | re | mi | fa | sol |
|---|---|---|---|---|---|---|---|---|
| *Frets* | 0 | 1 | 2 | 3 | 4 | 5 | 6 | 7 |
| *Note names for D* *Mixolydian scale* | D | E | F♯ | G | A | B | C | D |

Here is the traditional way to tune the dulcimer to play tunes with a Mixolydian melody in D:

TUNING TO **D** *bass string*
**A** *middle string*
**D'** *treble string(s)*

 Ex.43

1. Tune the bass string to low D (or pick a random note to tune the dulcimer to itself, and follow the next two steps.)

2. Fret the bass string at the 4th fret and tune the open middle string to sound the same as the fretted bass string.

3. Now, fret the *MIDDLE* string at the 3rd fret and tune the open treble string(s) to sound the same as the fretted middle string. The treble string(s) are tuned higher for this tuning than any of the others. D' means high D. It's an octave above the open bass string.

You're tuned to these notes:

On the piano:

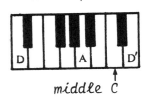

*middle C*

On the guitar:

D         A         D'

## THREE EASY WAYS TO ENHANCE TUNES IN $\begin{smallmatrix}D\\A\\D'\end{smallmatrix}$ TUNING USING PARALLEL CHORDS

### 1. TREBLE/MIDDLE STRING PARALLEL CHORDS

If you're playing a melody on the treble string(s), try fretting the middle string one fret higher than the treble string(s) to get a harmony part. Remember that the Mixolydian scale has a slightly different sound than the Ionian scale because of its lowered 7th tone. Try using your index finger on the middle string and your ring finger on the treble string(s).

```
bass   drone    —0—0—0—0—0—0—0—0—0—0—0—0—0—0—0—
middle harmony —3—4—5—6—7—8—9—10—11—12—13—14—15—16—17—
treble melody  —2—3—4—5—6—7—8—9—10—11—12—13—14—15—16—
```

### 2. MORE TREBLE/MIDDLE STRING PARALLEL CHORDS

Try fretting the middle string two frets below the treble string(s) and you will find another harmony. Try using your middle or ring finger on the middle string and either your thumb or index finger on the treble string(s).

```
bass   drone   —0—0—0—0—0—0—0—0—0—0—0—0—0—0—0—0—0-
middle harmony —1—2—3—4—5—6—7—8—9—10—11—12—13—14—15—16—17-
treble melody  —3—4—5—6—7—8—9—10—11—12—13—14—15—16—17—18—19-
```

### 3. BASS/MIDDLE STRING PARALLEL CHORDS

Since the treble string(s) and the bass string are tuned to the same note in $\begin{smallmatrix}D\\A\\D'\end{smallmatrix}$ tuning, you can easily play the melody on the bass string since the fret numbers will be the same. Using the bass string instead of the treble string(s) for the melody, try the same harmony given at the top of the page. For fingering, try using your ring or middle finger on the bass string and your index finger on the middle string.

```
bass   melody  —2—3—4—5—6—7—8—9—10—11—12—13—14—15—16—17-
middle harmony —3—4—5—6—7—8—9—10—11—12—13—14—15—16—17—18-
treble drone   —0—0—0—0—0—0—0—0—0—0—0—0—0—0—0—0-
```

Let your ear be your guide in choosing harmony parts. Sometimes you will need to alter them to suit the song. Also remember that often two-finger chords sound odd by themselves but when played in the context of the song, they sound fine.

## BARRE CHORDS

If you fret the same fret across all the strings, you get a *barre* chord.
Here are two ways to finger *barre* chords:

### USING THREE FINGERS TO MAKE A BARRE CHORD

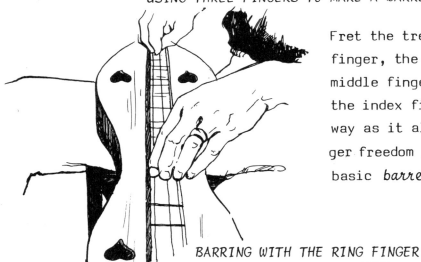

Fret the treble string(s) with the ring finger, the middle string with the middle finger, and the bass string with the index finger. I prefer the first way as it allows the thumb and ring finger freedom to add melody notes from the basic *barre* chord position.

### BARRING WITH THE RING FINGER

Fret all the strings with the ring finger. The middle finger can be placed on top of the ring finger to help press down the strings. The index finger or thumb can be used somewhat to play notes above the *barre*.

## BARRE CHORDS IN $_A^D$ $_{D'}$

If you make *barre* chords up the fretboard in $_A^D$ $_{D'}$, each fret position will give you a chord that can be used as either a major or minor. The note which distinguishes major from minor is missing from the chord.

| Chord names | E | F♯ | G | A | B | C | C♯ | D | E | etc. (These can be |
|---|---|---|---|---|---|---|---|---|---|---|
| bass string | 1 | 2 | 3 | 4 | 5 | 6 | 6½ | 7 | 8 | either major |
| middle string | 1 | 2 | 3 | 4 | 5 | 6 | 6½ | 7 | 8 | or minor.) |
| treble string(s) | 1 | 2 | 3 | 4 | 5 | 6 | 6½ | 7 | 8 | |

## SOME NEW CHORDS IN $_A^D$ $_{D'}$

### D CHORDS

| | | | | | |
|---|---|---|---|---|---|
| 0 | 0 | 2 | 4 | 7 | 0 |
| 5 | 3 | 3 | 5 | 7 | 5 |
| 4 | 2 | 0 | 0 | 0 | 7 |

### A CHORD

1
0
1

This arrangement of *Old Joe Clark* uses some of the parallel chords you've just learned for $\frac{D}{A}$ tuning. Try out the suggested fingering in the first few measures. If you prefer, $D'$ you can substitute the middle finger for the index finger on the middle string and the index finger for the thumb on the treble string(s). 

## Old Joe Clark
*Mixolydian Mode*

arr. Larkin Bryant

2. Old Joe Clark he had a dog, blind as he could be,
   Chased a bedbug 'round a stump and a snake up a holler tree. CHORUS

3. Wish I was in Tennessee, sittin' in a big armchair,
   One arm 'round my whiskey jar, and another one 'round my dear. CHORUS

Copyright © 1982 **IVORY PALACES Music** Publishing Company, Inc. 3141 Spottswood Avenue • Memphis, Tennessee • 38111
All rights reserved, including the right to photocopy.

74

This arrangement of *Harrison Town* uses D A D' parallel chords extensively (see p.72). To retain the modal flavor of this tune, the C chord 0 6 6 retains the D drone in the bass. ◨

# Harrison Town 1
### Mixolydian Mode (melody on treble string(s))

arr. Larkin Bryant

D A D' tuning

2.  As I rode down to Harrison town a couple of days ago,
    I turned my face toward the west to Eureka I did go;
    That Harrison crowd that followed me, they knew I'd have no doubt
    That I would lie in the Berryville jail before the week was out.

Copyright © 1982 **IVORY PALACES** Music Publishing Company, Inc. 3141 Spottswood Avenue • Memphis, Tennessee • 38111
All rights reserved, including the right to photocopy.

Harrison Town 2 can be played as a duet part by another dulcimer or as a variation of Harrison Town 1. In Harrison Town 2 the melody switches to the bass string using bass/middle string DAD' parallel chords (see p. 72).

# Harrison Town 2
### Mixolydian Mode (melody on bass string)

arr. Larkin Bryant

3. They took me down to Berryville, boys, I went through courts of law,
   I took my ride by the marshal's side to Little Rock, Arkansas;
   Oh, listen all you gambling boys, hear what stands over my case,
   It's the big grey horse, a noble horse, that I rode in the race.

Copyright © 1982 IVORY PALACES Music Publishing Company, Inc. 3141 Spottswood Avenue • Memphis, Tennessee • 38111
All rights reserved, including the right to photocopy.

## HISTORICAL NOTES

### MORNING SONG

*Morning Song* was first printed in *Kentucky Harmony* which was compiled and published by Ananias Davis, a Presbyterian singing master of Harrisonburg, Virginia. *Kentucky Harmony,* a shape-note collection published in 1816, was the first hymnal printed in the South.   The tune, *Morning Song,* is attributed to Mr. Dean.

### SIMPLE GIFTS

This rather lively Shaker song appeared in many collections as early as 1837 and was sung everywhere in the United Shaker Society.   Shakers, who lived in communities apart from regular society, had special dances and songs that they used in religious ceremonies.   This song reflects the theme of simplicity, one of the most pervasive of Shaker virtues.

### BRAHMS LULLABY (WIEGENLIED Op.49, No.4)

Brahms wrote *Wiegenlied* in 1868 for the first child of Berta Porubszy Faber. Before she married, Mrs. Faber had been a member of the choir that Brahms conducted in Hamburg.   Brahms later suggested that there should be a special edition of the lullaby in a minor key for naughty children.

### BALLADS

A ballad is a narrative story set to music.   In Anglo-American tradition, ballads tend to be highly romantic and sentimental, often dealing with the themes of love and death.   When a ballad enters into folk tradition it is transmitted orally from singer to singer, ofter undergoing textual changes as verses are lost, gained or altered.

* See Bibliography,  p. 103.

## PLAYING IONIAN MELODY SONGS IN D/A/D' TUNING

There is only one note that is different in the Ionian and Mixolydian modes and that is the 7th tone of the scale. Otherwise, the two scales are alike. This is important to you as a dulcimer player because many Ionian tunes omit the 7th tone of the scale. These Ionian tunes can be played in D/A/D' as well as D/A/A, but you'll have to use different fret numbers to play the melody and the chords.

*Attention dulcimer players with 6½ fret:* If you have the 6½ fret, you can play *any* Ionian mode song in D/A/D' because the 6½ fret is equal to the 7th tone of the Ionian scale. Try the two scales to see how it works.

> *Mixolydian mode fret numbers:* 0 1 2 3 4 5 6 7
>
> *Ionian mode starting from Mixolydian position:* 0 1 2 3 4 5 6½ 7

### WHAT DO YOU DO WHEN THE MELODY GOES BELOW THE OPEN TREBLE STRING(S)?

This is a pretty common occurrence in D/A/D' tuning because the scale begins at the open treble string(s). One thing you can do is play the low notes on the ba string.

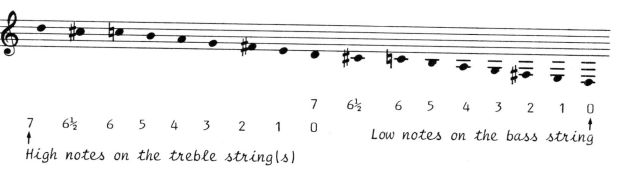

7 6½ 6 5 4 3 2 1 0      7 6½ 6 5 4 3 2 1 0

High notes on the treble string(s)      Low notes on the bass string

### SOME NEW D/A/D' CHORDS

D CHORDS

0 0 0
0 3 5
4 4 7

G CHORDS

3 3
3 3
3 5

*Cripple Creek* is an example of an Ionian melody played in $^D_A$ tuning (see p.78). The arrangement contains hammered notes and pull offs, plus $^{D'}$ *barre* chords and use of the bass string for some melody notes. Note that the tablature doesn't repeat every syllable of the words. This is common in fiddle tunes. If you strum every syllable of a word it sounds too cluttered. 🔲🔲

# Cripple Creek

*Ionian mode*

arr. Larkin Bryant

Copyright © 1982 **IVORY PALACES** Music Publishing Company, Inc. 3141 Spottswood Avenue • Memphis, Tennessee • 38111
All rights reserved, including the right to photocopy.

goin' in a whirl, Goin' up Cripple Creek to see my girl.

1.   I got á gal at the head of the creek,
     Go up to see her 'bout the middle of the week.
     Kiss on the mouth just as sweet as wine,
     Wraps herself around me like a sweet potato vine.

Chorus:
     Goin' up Cripple Creek, goin' in a run,
     Goin' up Cripple Creek to have some fun.
     Goin' up Cripple Creek, goin' in a whirl,
     Goin' up Cripple Creek to see my girl.

2.   Cripple Creek's wide and Cripple Creek's deep,
     Wade ol' Cripple Creek 'fore I sleep.
     Roads are rocky and the hillside's muddy,
     I'm so drunk I can't stand steady.

## THE PINCH: A TECHNIQUE FOR THE PICKING HAND

When you pluck more than one string at a time in fingerpicking, you're doing a pinch.  Pluck the strings with the same fingers you use for fingerpicking patterns.

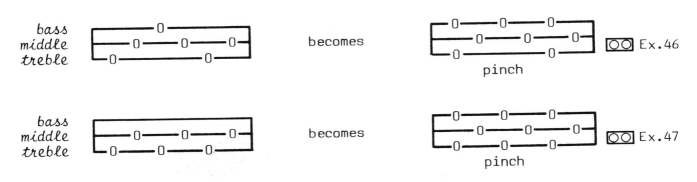

Middle finger/bass string
Index finger/middle string
Thumb/treble string(s)

## USING THE PINCH IN FOLKSTYLE PICKING PATTERNS

The pinch technique can replace plucking single strings in any picking pattern.  Here are some examples of the pinch used in picking patterns you already know.

Watch for pinches that are used with other picking patterns in the tablature that's coming up next.  Any of the picking patterns in $\frac{4}{4}$ or $\frac{3}{4}$ time can be shortened to fit a measure of $\frac{2}{4}$ time.

## PLAYING MELODY ON THE MIDDLE STRING

When you are fingerpicking and playing chords, it's easy to play some of the melody notes on the middle string because they happen to be present in the chord position being played. Here are two examples from *Amazing Grace* and *Down Came An Angel*. The melody notes are circled.

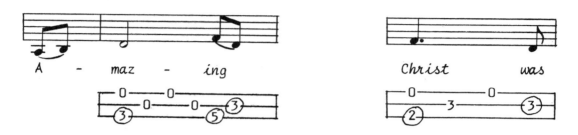

## BREAKING THE FLOW OF FOLKSTYLE PICKING PATTERNS

To add some interest to a folkstyle fingerpicking arrangement, you can leave out some of the non-melody notes in the picking patterns. An example of this technique is shown in these measures from *Down Came An Angel*. An "x" indicates the notes in the pattern that are left out.

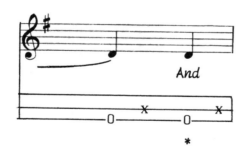

Down Came An Angel uses the pinch technique with some of the picking patterns. You'll notice that some of the melody notes are played on the middle string, and the C chord has a D drone in the bass.

# Down Came An Angel

Mixolydian Mode

arr. Larkin Bryant

Copyright © 1982 **IVORY PALACES** Music Publishing Company, Inc. 3141 Spottswood Avenue • Memphis, Tennessee • 38111

All rights reserved, including the right to photocopy.

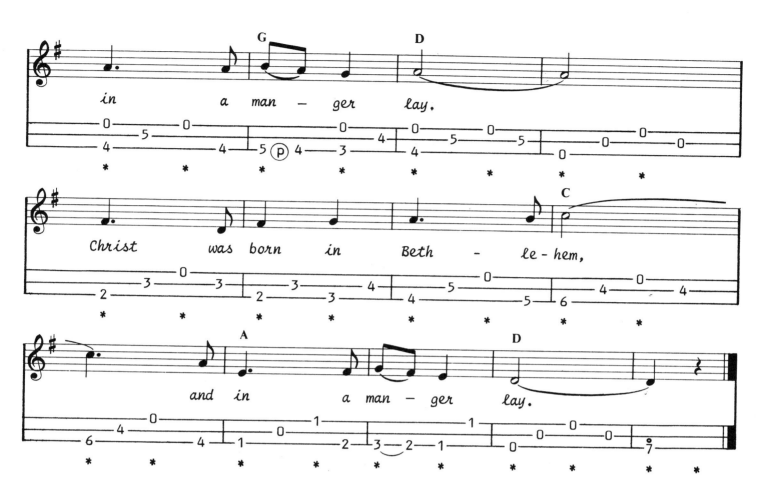

in a man - ger lay.

Christ was born in Beth - le - hem,

and in a man - ger lay.

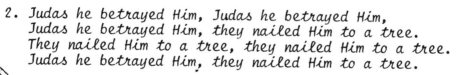

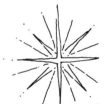

2. Judas he betrayed Him, Judas he betrayed Him,
   Judas he betrayed Him, they nailed Him to a tree.
   They nailed Him to a tree, they nailed Him to a tree.
   Judas he betrayed Him, they nailed Him to a tree.

3. Joseph begged His body, Joseph begged His body,
   Joseph begged His body, they laid Him in a tomb.
   They laid Him in a tomb, they laid Him in a tomb.
   Joseph begged His body, they laid Him in a tomb.

4. The tomb it would not hold Him, the tomb it would not hold Him,
   The tomb it would not hold Him, He burst the bonds of death.
   He burst the bonds of death, He burst the bonds of death.
   The tomb it would not hold Him, He burst the bonds of death.

5. Down came an angel, down came an angel,
   Down came an angel, and rolled the stone away.
   And rolled the stone away, and rolled the stone away.
   Down came an angel, and rolled the stone away.

Amazing Grace is the last arrangement of folkstyle fingerpicking in the book. You'll find picking patterns with the pinch technique, three finger chords, and examples of the melody played on the middle string as well as on the treble string(s). You might want to go over the three finger chords before playing the tune.

# Amazing Grace

Ionian Mode

arr. Larkin Bryant

Copyright © 1982 IVORY PALACES Music Publishing Company, Inc.  3141 Spottswood Avenue • Memphis, Tennessee • 38111
All rights reserved, including the right to photocopy.

1. Amazing grace (how sweet the sound)
   That sav'd a wretch like me!
   I once was lost, but now am found,
   Was blind, but now I see.

2. 'Twas grace that taught my heart to fear,
   And grace my fear relieved;
   How precious did that grace appear,
   The hour I first believed!

3. Thro' many dangers, toils and snares,
   I have already come;
   'Tis grace has brought me safe thus far,
   And grace will bring me home.

4. The Lord has promised good to me,
   His word my hope secures:
   He will my shield and portion be
   As long as life endures.

5. When we've been there ten thousand years,
   Bright shining as the sun,
   We've no less days to sing God's praise
   Than when we've first begun.

### SOME THREE FINGER CHORDS IN D A A TUNING

| D CHORDS | | G CHORD | A CHORDS | | A7 CHORD | Bm CHORDS | |
|---|---|---|---|---|---|---|---|
| 4I | 7I | 3I | 4I | 4I | 4I | 2I | 5I |
| 3R | 5L* | 1L | 2L | 4M | 4M | 1L | 3L |
| 5T | 7T | 3T | 4T | 7T | 6T | 3T | 5T |

* L means little finger.

## CLASSICAL STYLE FINGERPICKING

Classical style dulcimer is similar in sound to lute and classical guitar playing. Many finger techniques such as hammered notes, pull offs, slides, pinches, and drags make up the essence of this style. It's quite different in sound from the even, flowing rhythm of folkstyle picking patterns.

## THE DRAG: A TECHNIQUE FOR THE PICKING HAND

The drag is the opposite of the brush (see p.48). It's done by slowly dragging the index finger of the picking hand across all the strings from bass to treble. You should do the drag slowly enough to hear the sound of each individual string (sounds like ba-da-dum). 🔲 Ex.48

```
                                      0                        0
              written like this:  0       sounds like this:  0
                                      0                            0
```

## INTERPRETATION OF CLASSICAL STYLE FINGERPICKING TABLATURE

When you see three fret numbers stacked vertically $\begin{smallmatrix}0\\0\\0\end{smallmatrix}$ , you can play them as a drag, a pinch or a brush. They are interchangable and using them is a matter of personal style.

As a general rule in chording and picking, leave the fingers in a chord position until you have to move them to play another position. Holding the chords as long as you can allows the strings to ring, sustaining and giving continuity to the overall sound.

## NEW CHORDS IN $\begin{smallmatrix}D\\A\\C\end{smallmatrix}$

| Dm CHORDS | | Am CHORD | Gm CHORD |
|---|---|---|---|
| 0 | 0 | 1 | 3 ı |
| 0 | 3 | 0 | 3 м |
| 3 | 5 | 2 | 4 т |

# Morning Song
## Aeolian Mode

arr. Larkin Bryant

DAC tuning

2. Night unto night his name repeats,
   The day renews the sound;
   Wide as the heav'n on which he sits,
   To turn the seasons round.
   Wide as the heav'n on which he sits,
   To turn the seasons round.

Copyright © 1982 **IVORY PALACES** Music Publishing Company, Inc. 3141 Spottswood Avenue • Memphis, Tennessee • 38111
All rights reserved, including the right to photocopy.

88

Watch the timing on this one and practice it slowly until you feel comfortable playing it.

# Simple Gifts
## Ionian Mode

arr. Larkin Bryant

Copyright © 1982 IVORY PALACES Music Publishing Company, Inc. 3141 Spottswood Avenue • Memphis, Tennessee • 38111
All rights reserved, including the right to photocopy.

The following arrangement can be fingerpicked or flatpicked. In flatpicking, a medium to heavy guitar pick is used to pick individual strings as well as strumming across all strings. Look out for melody notes played on the middle and bass string as well as the treble string(s).

# Brahms' Lullaby

### Ionian Mode

arr. Larkin Bryant

D
A tuning
A

1. Lul-la-by and good night, with ros-es be-dight; With lil-ies be-decked is ba-by's wee bed; Lay thee down now and rest, May thy slum-ber be blest; Lay thee down now and rest, May thy slum-ber be blest.

2. *Lullaby and good night, thy mother's delight;*
   *Bright angels around my darling shall stand;*
   *They will guard thee from harms,*
   *Thou shalt wake in my arms;*
   *They will guard thee from harms,*
   *Thou shalt wake in my arms.*

Copyright © 1982 **IVORY PALACES Music** Publishing Company, Inc. 3141 Spottswood Avenue • Memphis, Tennessee • 38111
All rights reserved, including the right to photocopy.

# Appendix

### ABOUT MUSICAL TIME

Understanding how musical time values (rhythms) are written out is not too difficult if you think of them in terms of those pies that are divided up into slices. In fact, time values are "easy as pie" when you get right down to it! These are the notes to learn.

o whole note   ♩ half note   ♩ quarter note   ♪ eighth note   ♪ sixteenth note

These notes always have the same relationship to each other. Let's look at the pies to illustrate this. Each circle equals one whole pie and each slice represents a note.

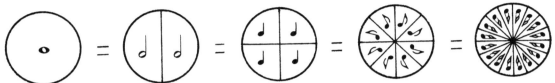

1 whole equals   2 halves equals   4 quarters equals   8 eighths equals   16 sixteenths

### LEARN THESE RELATIONSHIPS!

All time values which take up the same amount of pie are equal to each other.

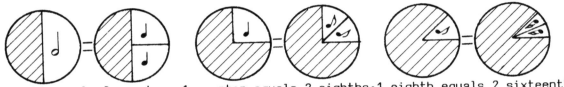

1 half equals 2 quarters•1 quarter equals 2 eighths•1 eighth equals 2 sixteenths

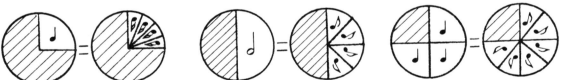

1 quarter equals 4 sixteenths•1 half equals 4 eighths•3 quarters equals 6 eighths

On occasion you will see a note with a dot after it. This means that the time value of that note has been increased by ½. For example:

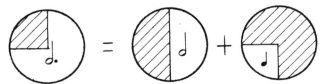

1 dotted half equals   1 half   plus   1 quarter

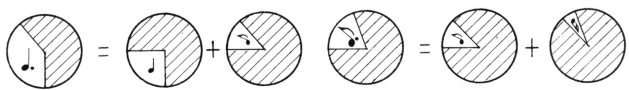

1 dotted quarter equals 1 quarter plus 1 eighth•1 dotted eighth equals 1 eighth plus 1 sixteenth

Copyright © 1982 **IVORY PALACES** Music Publishing Company, Inc. 3141 Spottswood Avenue • Memphis, Tennessee • 38111
All rights reserved, including the right to photocopy.

## THE BEAT

The beat is the natural, basic rhythm of a tune. You can clap your hands or tap your toe to this rhythmical beat. Toe tapping is an important part of playing traditional folk music. The percussive tones of a tapping foot add another "instrument" to the music. The beats are marked in the dulcimer tablature by an asterisk (*) to show you where to pat your foot and to help you with the rhythm.

## TIME SIGNATURES AND MEASURES

When music is written down, the beats are grouped into measures and each measure usually contains the same number of beats. The top number of the *time signature* at the beginning of the music notation tells you how many beats are in each measure.

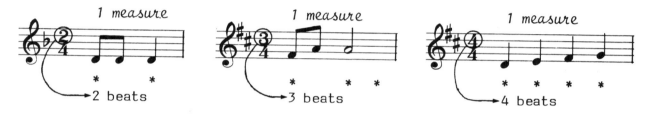

Sometimes the beginning measure of a song will be incomplete. You can tell this by looking at the number of beat marks and the time signature.

The bottom number of the *time signature* tells you what note will get one beat. All the time signatures in this book have a 4 on the bottom, which means that a quarter note ♩ gets 1 beat. By looking at the previous page you can see that if a quarter note gets one beat, then:

a half note ♩ gets 2 beats

an eighth note ♪ gets ½ beat

two eighth notes ♫ get 1 beat

one dotted quarter ♩. gets 1½ beats

a dotted quarter plus one eighth ♩.♪ gets 2 beats

## HOW TO READ THE DULCIMER TABLATURE

The tuning for the dulcimer strings is on the left side of each song title. See the tuning pages for instructions on each tuning (pp. 12, 40, 58 and 71).

The mode of each song is listed below the song title.

All modes in *Larkin's Dulcimer Book* are pitched in D and have the following key signatures:

        D  Ionian has two sharps:

        D  Dorian has no sharps or flats:

        D  Aeolian has one flat:

        D  Mixolydian has one sharp:

Every song has the melody written in music notation but fills (p. 34), strumming rhythms and dulcimer chords are found only in the tablature.

Chord names for an accompanying instrument are given above the music notation.

The numbers below the music notation are fret numbers for the dulcimer (see p. 5). If the tablature has a single row of fret numbers, this means that you play the melody on the treble string(s) while strumming the open middle and bass strings. If the tablature has three rows of fret numbers under the music notation, read the rows like this:

    top row:   bass string fret numbers
  middle row:  middle string fret numbers
  bottom row:  treble string(s) fret numbers

Sometimes fingering is suggested in the tablature. These abbreviations are:

    T (Thumb)   I (Index)  M (Middle)  R (Ring)  L (Little)

Here are the symbols for various finger techniques used in the tablature:

        Pull off (p)  (p. 55, 56)
        Hammer on (h)  (p. 53, 54)
        Slide ⌣  (p. 57)
        Harmonic °  (p. 57)

The strum guides (dots and dashes) under the treble string(s) fret numbers are explained on pages 15-21 and 31.

Folkstyle fingerpicking tablature is explained on page 47.

Classical style fingerpicking tablature is explained on page 87.

The asterisk (*) beneath the fret numbers shows you where the beat falls in each measure. Since the written measures are of varying lengths, the asterisks may be closer together or further apart in some measures, but even so, the beats are always steady.

## PLAYING BACK-UP CHORDS TO ACCOMPANY OTHER INSTRUMENTS OR VOICE

You can use the dulcimer to accompany another instrument or voice by playing back-up chords. The chord names above the music notation tell you what chords to play, and there are usually several fret positions for each chord in a tuning. When you are playing back-up chords, it doesn't matter which chord position you choose. However, if you choose chord positions that are close together on the fretboard, it makes back-up playing easier.

As an example, let's say that you want to play a tune in D that calls for D, G, A and B minor chords. It's a major sounding (Ionian) tune so you decide to choose $\begin{smallmatrix}D\\A\\A\end{smallmatrix}$ . Look at the chord charts for $\begin{smallmatrix}D\\A\\A\end{smallmatrix}$ to see if you have all the chords you need in that tuning. If the chords aren't possible in that tuning, check the chords in another one. Sometimes you won't be able to make certain chords in any of the tunings because of the dulcimer fret scale, in which case you'll have to "fake it." D,G,A and Bm chords are shown below grouped according to their location on the fretboard.

CHORD NAMES:
```
            D   G   A   Bm      D   G   A   Bm      D   G   A   Bm       D    G   A   Bm
        D—  2 — 3 — 1 — 2 ——— 4 — 5 — 4 — 5 ——— 7 — 7 — 4 — 7 ——— 9 — 10 — 8 — 9 —
        A—  0 — 1 — 0 — 1 ——— 3 — 3 — 2 — 3 ——— 5 — 6 — 4 — 5 ——— 7 — 8 — 7 — 8 —
        A—  3 — 3 — 2 — 3 ——— 5 — 6 — 4 — 5 ——— 7 — 8 — 7 — 8 ——— 10-10 — 9 —10—
```
*Location on the fretboard:*     *low*          *lower middle*      *upper middle*        *high*

If you're playing a fast fiddle tune in $\frac{2}{4}$ time, choose one of the strumming patterns or a combination of strumming patterns. If you're playing a pretty ballad choose a picking pattern or a combination of picking patterns in the appropriate time signature (i.e. walking beat: $\frac{2}{4}$ or $\frac{4}{4}$ ; waltz time: $\frac{3}{4}$ ). Consider also the classical style.

If you're wondering what instruments might be good for backing up, here are some ideas: flute, recorder, fiddle, mandolin, melody style autoharp, lead acoustic guitar, frailing style banjo. If your musician friend can read music, he or she can follow the music notation in the tablature in the book. That's 23 tunes you could play! And you can play back-up chords for other keys by referring to the chord charts on pages 96-100.

Be sure you are tuned together by matching the tone of your open middle string (A) with the A on your friend's instrument. Once your A's are together, you can re-tune your bass string (if necessary) by matching the sound of the 4th fret on your bass string to your open middle string. Then tune your treble string(s) to whatever mode you want.

## TUNING THE DULCIMER TO PLAY IN OTHER KEYS

When you play by yourself, it doesn't matter what notes you're tuned to as long as you're in some kind of tuning.  There will be times, such as a jam session, when you'll want to play in different keys.  The dulcimer can actually be played in any key, but it takes a certain knowledge of the instrument to be able to do this.  Theoretically, you could take the tunings in this book and pitch them for any key.  This wouldn't work in reality, however, because your strings would have to be tuned too high or too low for some of the keys.  For this reason, many new tunings for the modes have been developed in recent years. By chording (see p. 101, 102) and using the capo, you can also play in different modes and keys in each tuning.

The tunings in *Larkin's Dulcimer Book* can be raised or lowered several steps in pitch to allow you to play in the keys of C, E and F as well as D without tuning too low or too high.  Page 101 has instructions for tuning to these keys.

## RAISING OR LOWERING A TUNING TO C, E, OR F

When you raise or lower the entire pitch of a tuning, the fret numbers of the chords do not change.  However, the *names* of the chords  *do* change. For example: when tuned to $^{D}_{A}_{A}$, the chord position $^{2}_{0}_{3}$ is called a D chord.  If you lower the pitch of $^{D}_{A}_{A}$ tuning to $^{A}_{C}_{G}$ $^{C}_{G}$... the same $^{2}_{0}_{3}$ chord position becomes a C chord.  Look at the chart below to see how chord names change.*

| chord names in D: (as listed in the chord charts) | D | E | F | F♯ | G | G♯(A♭) | A | B♭ | B | C | C♯ |
|---|---|---|---|---|---|---|---|---|---|---|---|
| | | | *tunings raised to 'E' (see p. 101)* | | | | | | | | |
| chord names become: | E | F♯ | G | G♯ | A | A♯ | B | C | C♯ | D | D♯ |
| | | | | *tunings raised to 'F' (see p. 101)* | | | | | | | |
| chord names become: | F | G | A♭ | A | B♭ | B | C | D♭ | D | E♭ | E |
| | | | | *tunings raised to 'C' (see p. 101)* | | | | | | | |
| chord names become: | C | D | E♭ | E | F | G♭ | G | A♭ | A | B♭ | B |

* Names may represent either major, minor or 7th chords; refer to chord charts for fret positions.

## SOME CHORDS FOR D A D' TUNING

+ means complete chords (triads); all others are incomplete. Incomplete chords which can be either major or minor are indicated by Ø. Incomplete chords with a missing root are indicated by x.

D
D7
Dmaj7
Dm
Dm7
E
E7
Em
Em7
F
Fm
F♯
F♯7
F♯m
F♯m7
G
Gmaj7
Gm
G♯
G♯m
A
A7
Amaj7
Am
Am7
B
B7
Bm
Bm7
C
Cmaj7
Cm
C♯
C♯7
C♯m7
D
A
D'

Copyright © 1982 IVORY PALACES Music Publishing Company, Inc. 3141 Spottswood Avenue • Memphis, Tennessee • 38111
All rights reserved, including the right to photocopy.

## SOME CHORDS FOR $^D_A_C$ TUNING

+ means complete chords (triads); all others are incomplete. Incomplete chords which can be either major or minor are indicated by Ø. Incomplete chords with a missing root are indicated by x.

```
         D                              D⁷              Dmaj⁷ Dm                    Dm⁷
D —0—2—0—0—7—7—7—9—9┌0—0—0—7—7—6┌2—9┌0—0—4—0—7—7—11┌0—6—7—
A —0—0—3—5—5—7—7—7—10│0—5—5—5—7—5│2—9│0—0—3—3—7—7—10│0—3—7—
C —1—1—5—5—5—5—8—8—12└0—0—7—7—7—8└1—8└1—3—3—5—5—8—10└0—3—7—

   Ø  +  Ø  +  +  Ø  Ø  +  +  Ø        Ø        Ø  +  +  Ø  Ø  Ø  +  Ø   Ø
```

```
   Eᵇ   E         E⁷      Em              Em⁷           F   Fm    F♯
D —3┌1—5—8—5—8┌1—8—8┌1—3—5—8—8—10┌1—8—8┌6—6—6—6┌2—6½—
A —6│1—6½—6½—6½—8│1—6½—8│1—1—4—6—8—8│1—6—8│0—7│6½—6½│2—5—
C —6│2—6½—6½—9—9│1—8—8│2—2—4—6½—9—9│1—8—8│3—10│7—10│6—6—

   x    Ø   x   +  +  Ø  Ø  Ø  Ø  +  +  +  Ø  +  Ø    Ø    +  +  x  +   +  +
```

```
   F♯    F♯⁷  F♯maj⁷ F♯m        F♯m⁷    G              G⁷
D —6½—9┌2—2┌2—2—6½—9—11┌2—9┌0—3—5—3—0—10—7┌3—3—0—7—10—10—
A —9—9│2—4│2—2—5—9—9│0—7│1—3—3—3—6—8—8│1—3—6—6—10—8—
C —6—13│2—6│3—5—5—12—12│2—9│4—4—4—6½—8—8│3—3—3—10—10—10—

   x   +  Ø       +  +  +  x         +  Ø  +  Ø  +  +  Ø  Ø  Ø  Ø
```

```
   Gm              Gm⁷        Aᵇ Aᵇm Aᵇm⁷ A               A⁷
D —3—3—0—7—0—10┌3—0—7—10┌6½┌5┌9┌1—4—4—4—6½—8—11┌4—4—11—
A —3—3—6—10—6—10│3—6—6—10│6½│6½│6½│0—0—2—4—9—7—9│4—2—9—
C —4—6—6—6—8—13│3—3—10—10│7│6½│6½│2—2—2—5—9—9—12│4—4—11—

   Ø  +  +  x  Ø  +  Ø  Ø  Ø  Ø       Ø  Ø  +  Ø  x  Ø   Ø
```

```
   Am                    Am⁷   Bᵇ  Bᵇm    B    B⁷    Bm
D —1—4—1—4—4—6—8—8┌4—7┌6½—6½┌5—9┌5—9—9┌2—5—7—9—5—9—
A —0—4—0—0—4—4—7—7│4│4│10│9—9│5—8│5—7—8│1—5—5—8—5—8—
C —0—0—2—2—5—5—7—9│4│4│6│6—10│6½—6½│5—6½—12│1—6½—6½—6½—8—8—

   +  +  Ø  Ø  Ø  +  +  Ø  Ø      x   Ø  Ø  Ø  Ø  +  Ø  +  Ø  +  +
```

```
   Bm⁷        C                    C⁷          Cm      Cm⁷  C♯
D —5—5—9—9┌3—6—6—6—10—6—13—13┌6—6—13┌6—6—13┌6┌6½—6½—
A —3—5—7—8│4—4—6—6—11—6—11—13│4—6—11│6—6—13│6│6½—9—
C —5—5—6½—12│0—4—4—7—7—9—11—11│6—6—13│4—7—11│6│10—10—

   Ø  Ø  Ø  +  +  Ø  Ø  +  +  +  Ø    Ø    Ø  Ø  Ø  Ø    +
```

```
   C♯m
D —6½—6½
A —6½—9
C —9—9

   +
```

```
D ————————
A ————————
C ————————
```

Copyright © 1982 **IVORY PALACES** Music Publishing Company, Inc. 3141 Spottswood Avenue • Memphis, Tennessee • 38111
All rights reserved, including the right to photocopy.

## SOME CHORDS FOR $\begin{smallmatrix}D\\A\\G\end{smallmatrix}$ TUNING

+ means complete chords (triads);   all others are incomplete.   Incomplete chords which can be either major or minor are indicated by Ø.   Incomplete chords with a missing root are indicated by x.

Copyright © 1982 **IVORY PALACES Music** Publishing Company, Inc.  3141 Spottswood Avenue • Memphis, Tennessee • 38111
All rights reserved, including the right to photocopy.

## SOME CHORDS FOR $\begin{smallmatrix}D\\A\\A\end{smallmatrix}$ TUNING

+ means complete chords (triads); all others are incomplete. Incomplete chords which can be either major or minor are indicated by Ø. Incomplete chords with a missing root are indicated by x.

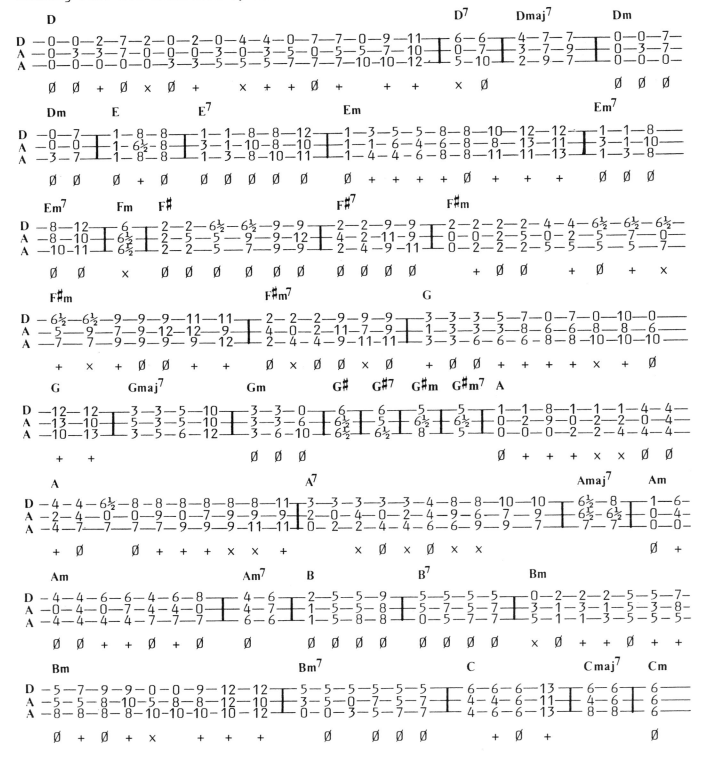

Copyright © 1982 **IVORY PALACES** Music Publishing Company, Inc. 3141 Spottswood Avenue • Memphis, Tennessee • 38111
All rights reserved, including the right to photocopy.

```
        C#        C#7         C#m                                                      C#m7
D — 6½  |   6½ - 6½  |  1—1—6½—6½—8—8—8—8—8  |  5— 6½— 6½
A — 6½  |   8 - 6½   |  2—2—4—6½—9—9—6½-9—11 |  4— 8— 6½
A — 6½  |   6½ - 8   |  2—4—6½—6½—9—6½-9—11—9|  2— 6½— 8
     Ø        Ø    Ø        +   Ø    +   +          Ø   Ø
```

## FRET CHART FOR MAKING YOUR OWN CHORDS

### D A A Tuning

| frets | 0 | 1 | 2 | 3 | 4 | 5 | 6 | 6½ | 7 | 8 | 9 | 10 | 11 | 12 | 13 | 13½ | 14 | 15 | 16 | 17 | 18 |
|---|---|---|---|---|---|---|---|---|---|---|---|---|---|---|---|---|---|---|---|---|---|
| D | D | E | F# | G | A | B | C | C# | D | E | F# | G | A | B | C | C# | D | E | F# | G | A |
| A | A | B | C# | D | E | F# | G | G# | A | B | C# | D | E | F# | G | G# | A | B | C# | D | E |
| A | A | B | C# | D | E | F# | G | G# | A | B | C# | D | E | F# | G | G# | A | B | C# | D | E |
|  | 0 | 1 | 2 | 3 | 4 | 5 | 6 | 6½ | 7 | 8 | 9 | 10 | 11 | 12 | 13 | 13½ | 14 | 15 | 16 | 17 | 18 |

### D A G Tuning

| | 0 | 1 | 2 | 3 | 4 | 5 | 6 | 6½ | 7 | 8 | 9 | 10 | 11 | 12 | 13 | 13½ | 14 | 15 | 16 | 17 | 18 |
|---|---|---|---|---|---|---|---|---|---|---|---|---|---|---|---|---|---|---|---|---|---|
| D | D | E | F# | G | A | B | C | C# | D | E | F# | G | A | B | C | C# | D | E | F# | G | A |
| A | A | B | C# | D | E | F# | G | G# | A | B | C# | D | E | F# | G | G# | A | B | C# | D | E |
| G | G | A | B | C | D | E | F | F# | G | A | B | C | D | E | F | F# | G | A | B | C | D |
|  | 0 | 1 | 2 | 3 | 4 | 5 | 6 | 6½ | 7 | 8 | 9 | 10 | 11 | 12 | 13 | 13½ | 14 | 15 | 16 | 17 | 18 |

### D A C Tuning

| | 0 | 1 | 2 | 3 | 4 | 5 | 6 | 6½ | 7 | 8 | 9 | 10 | 11 | 12 | 13 | 13½ | 14 | 15 | 16 | 17 | 18 |
|---|---|---|---|---|---|---|---|---|---|---|---|---|---|---|---|---|---|---|---|---|---|
| D | D | E | F# | G | A | B | C | C# | D | E | F# | G | A | B | C | C# | D | E | F# | G | A |
| A | A | B | C# | D | E | F# | G | G# | A | B | C# | D | E | F# | G | G# | A | B | C# | D | E |
| C | C | D | E | F | G | A | Bb | B | C | D | E | F | G | A | Bb | B | C | D | E | F | G |
|  | 0 | 1 | 2 | 3 | 4 | 5 | 6 | 6½ | 7 | 8 | 9 | 10 | 11 | 12 | 13 | 13½ | 14 | 15 | 16 | 17 | 18 |

### D A D' Tuning

| | 0 | 1 | 2 | 3 | 4 | 5 | 6 | 6½ | 7 | 8 | 9 | 10 | 11 | 12 | 13 | 13½ | 14 | 15 | 16 | 17 | 18 |
|---|---|---|---|---|---|---|---|---|---|---|---|---|---|---|---|---|---|---|---|---|---|
| D | D | E | F# | G | A | B | C | C# | D | E | F# | G | A | B | C | C# | D | E | F# | G | A |
| A | A | B | C# | D | E | F# | G | G# | A | B | C# | D | E | F# | G | G# | A | B | C# | D | E |
| D' | D' | E | F# | G | A | B | C | C# | D | E | F# | G | A | B | C | C# | D | E | F# | G | A |
|  | 0 | 1 | 2 | 3 | 4 | 5 | 6 | 6½ | 7 | 8 | 9 | 10 | 11 | 12 | 13 | 13½ | 14 | 15 | 16 | 17 | 18 |

Copyright © 1982 IVORY PALACES Music Publishing Company, Inc. 3141 Spottswood Avenue • Memphis, Tennessee • 38111
All rights reserved, including the right to photocopy.

## QUICK REFERENCE FOR MODES AND TUNINGS IN LARKIN'S DULCIMER BOOK

### MODES

*Ionian* - the major scale:  begins at the 3rd fret (any string) or at the open strings using the 6½ fret.

*Dorian* - a minor sounding scale:  begins at the 4th fret (any string) or at the 1st fret using the 6½ fret.

*Aeolian* - a minor sounding scale:  begins at the 1st fret (any string) or at the 5th fret using the 6½ fret.

*Mixolydian* - a major sounding scale:  begins at the open string (any string) or at the 4th fret using the 6½ fret.

### TUNINGS

All tunings in this book begin by:
1. Tuning the bass string to low D.
2. Tuning the middle string to sound the same as the 4th fret on the bass string.
3. Tuning the treble string(s) to one of the following:

*Tuning I*    D A A - Tune the treble string(s) to sound the same as the open middle string.

*Tuning II*   D A G - Tune the treble string(s) to sound the same as the 3rd fret on the bass string.

*Tuning III*  D A C - Tune the treble string(s) to sound the same as the 6th fret on the bass string.

*Tuning IV*   D A D'- Tune the treble string(s) to sound the same as the 3rd fret on the middle string.

### PLAYING IN THE KEYS OF C, E, AND F

The above tunings can be lowered or raised so you can play in C, E and F:

#### PLAYING IN C

Tune the bass string to low C, shown below.  Follow tuning steps 2 and 3 above.

C

*Tuning I:* C G G

*Tuning II:* C G F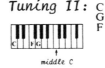

*Tuning III:* C G B♭

*Tuning IV:* C G C'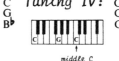

#### PLAYING IN E

Tune the bass string to low E, shown below.  Follow tuning steps 2 and 3 above.

E

*Tuning I:* E B B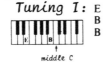

*Tuning II:* E B A

*Tuning III:* E B D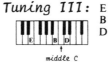

*Tuning IV:* E B E'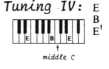

#### PLAYING IN F

Tune the bass string to low F, shown below.  Follow tuning steps 2 and 3 above.

F

*Tuning I:* F C C

*Tuning II:* F C B♭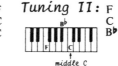

*Tuning III:* F C E♭

*Tuning IV:* F C F'

Copyright © 1982 **IVORY PALACES** Music Publishing Company, Inc.   3141 Spottswood Avenue • Memphis, Tennessee • 38111
All rights reserved, including the right to photocopy.

## POSSIBLE MODES AND KEYS IN D/A/A, D/A/G, D/A/C, D/A/D' TUNINGS

By chording and using the 6½ fret, many modes and keys are possible in the four tunings in *Larkin's Dulcimer Book.* You will have to play chords to harmonize modes that do not begin on D.

### D/A/A Tuning

| Key | Fret | Mode | |
|-----|------|------|---|
| D | 3 | D Ionian | |
| Em | 4 | E Dorian | |
| E | 4 | E Mixolydian | needs 6½ fret |
| F#m | 5 | F# Aeolian | needs 6½ fret |
| A | 0 | A Mixolydian | |
| A | 0 | A Ionian | needs 6½ fret |
| Bm | 1 | B Aeolian | |
| Bm | 1 | B Dorian | needs 6½ fret |

### D/A/G Tuning

| Key | Fret | Mode | |
|-----|------|------|---|
| Dm | 4 | D Dorian | |
| D | 4 | D Mixolydian | needs 6½ fret |
| Em | 5 | E Aeolian | needs 6½ fret |
| G | 0 | G Mixolydian | |
| G | 0 | G Ionian | needs 6½ fret |
| Am | 1 | A Aeolian | |
| Am | 1 | A Dorian | needs 6½ fret |

### D/A/C Tuning

| Key | Fret | Mode | |
|-----|------|------|---|
| Dm | 1 | D Aeolian | |
| Dm | 1 | D Dorian | needs 6½ fret |
| Gm | 4 | G Dorian | |
| G | 4 | G Mixolydian | needs 6½ fret |
| Am | 5 | A Aeolian | needs 6½ fret |

### D/A/D' Tuning

| Key | Fret | Mode | |
|-----|------|------|---|
| D | 0 | D Mixolydian | |
| D | 0 | D Ionian | needs 6½ fret |
| Em | 1 | E Aeolian | |
| Em | 1 | E Dorian | needs 6½ fret |
| G | 3 | G Ionian | |
| Am | 4 | A Dorian | |
| A | 4 | A Mixolydian | needs 6½ fret |
| Bm | 5 | B Aeolian | needs 6½ fret |

Copyright © 1982 **IVORY PALACES** Music Publishing Company, Inc. 3141 Spottswood Avenue • Memphis, Tennessee • 38111
All rights reserved, including the right to photocopy.

# BIBLIOGRAPHY

ANDREWS, Edward D. The Gift To Be Simple. New York: Dover Publications, 1962.

BELDON, H.M. Ballads and Songs Collected by the Missouri Folklore Society. Columbia, MO: University of Missouri Press, 1966.

BENZIGER, Barbara and DICKINSON, Eleanor. That Old Time Religion. New York: Harper & Row, 1975.

BOTKIN, B.A. The American Play-Party Song. New York: Ungar, 1963.

BROWN, Frank C. North Carolina Folklore, 5 vols. Vol. 3: Folk Songs of North Carolina. Durham, NC: Duke University Press, 1952.

CHASE, Richard. Old Songs and Singing Games. New York: Dover Publications, 1972.

CHILD, Francis. English and Scottish Popular Ballads. New York: Dover Publications, 1965.

COLCORD, Joanna. Roll and Go, Songs of American Sailormen. New York: W.W.Norton, 1938.

COX, Frederick. English Madrigals At the Time of Shakespeare. London: J.M.Dent, Aldine House, 1973.

COX, John H. Folk Songs Mainly From West Virginia. New York: Da Capo Press, 1977.

EATON, Allen. Handicrafts of the Southern Highlands. New York: Dover Publications, 1973.

ERBSEN, Wayne. Wayne Erbsen's Back Pocket Old Time Songbook. New York: Pembroke Music Co., Inc., 1981.

FULD, James J. The Book of World Famous Music. New York: Crown Publishers, 1971.

FORD, Ira. Traditional Music In America. Hatboro, PA: Folklore Associates, 1965.

CUNEY-HARE, Maud. Negro Musicians And Their Music. New York: Da Capo Press, 1974.

JACKSON, George P. White Spirituals of the Southern Uplands. Chapel Hill: University of North Carolina Press, 1933.

LOMAX, Alan. The Folk Songs of North America. Garden City, NY: Doubleday, 1960.

LOMAX, John and LOMAX, Alan. Our Singing Country. New York: Macmillan Co.,1938.

LORENZ, Ellen J. '76 to '76. Dayton, OH: Lorenz Publishing Co., 1975.

NAYLOR, Edward A.,ed. Shakespeare Music (Music of the Period). New York: Da Capo Press, 1973.

PERROW, E.C. "Songs and Rhymes From the South." Journal of American Folklore, Vol.26(1913):123-173.

RANDOLPH, Vance. Ozark Folksongs. 4 vols. Columbia, MO: The State Historical Society of Missouri, 1946-50.

REYNOLDS, W.J. Companion To the Baptist Hymnal. Nashville: Broadman Press, 1976.

RITCHIE, Jean. Carols Of All Seasons(liner notes to sound recording). Tradition Records, TLP 1031.

SADIE, Stanley, ed. The New Grove Dictionary of Music and Musicians. London: Macmillan Co., 1980.

SANDBURG, Carl. The American Songbag. New York: Harcourt, Brace, 1927.

SANDVED, Kjell Bloch, ed. The World of Music: An Illustrated Encyclopedia. New York: Abradale Press, 1963.

SCARBOROUGH, Dorothy. On The Trail Of Negro Folksongs. Hatboro, PA: Folklore Associates, 1963.

SCOTT, Sir Walter. Minstrelsy Of the Scottish Border: Vol. III. London: Adam and Charles Black.

The Hymnal 1940 Companion. Protestant Episcopal Church In the USA, New York: Church Pension Fund, 1951.

THOMAS, Jean and LEEDER, J.A. The Singin' Gathern': Tunes From the Southern Appalachians. New York: Silver Burdette Co., 1939.

WHITE, Newman. American Negro Folksongs. Hatboro, PA: Folklore Associates, 1965.

# ORDER FORM

## For

# Larkin's Dulcimer Book

(order form may be photocopied)

Date _____

Ship to:

Name_____ Phone___-__-_____

Address _____

City_____State_____Zip_____

Billing address if
different from above

Name_____ Phone___-__-_____

Address _____

City _____State_____ Zip_____

| Qty. | Page No. | Description | Price each | | Total | |
|------|----------|-------------|------------|-----|-------|-----|
| | | *Larkin's Dulcimer Book | $9 | 95 | | |
| | | *Companion Cassette | $7 | 98 | | |
| | | | | | | |
| | | | | | | |
| | | | | | | |
| | | | | | | |
| | | | | | | |
| | | | | | | |
| | | *Both book and tape together | $16 | 95 | | |
| | | Sub-total | | | | |
| | | Sales tax-Tennessee residents add 7% (or I.D. number if tax exempt) | | | | |
| | | postage and handling | | | $1 | 50 |
| | | | | | | |
| | | Total | | | | |

Make checks payable to: IVORY PALACES Music

(901)323-3509

Please allow 4-6 weeks for delivery.

Prices subject to change without notice.

IVORY PALACES Music Publishing Company, Inc. 3141 Spottswood Avenue • Memphis, Tennessee • 38111